S0-AHE-191

TEACHING COMPOSING

Robert W. Boynton — Consulting Editor

Former Principal, Senior High School
and Chairman, English Department
Germantown Friends School

TEACHING COMPOSING

William E. Coles, Jr.
Professor of English, Director of Composition
University of Pittsburgh

HAYDEN BOOK COMPANY, INC.
Rochelle Park, New Jersey

161872

808.04275
C 693t

For Theodore Baird

Library of Congress Cataloging in Publication Data

Coles, William E
  Teaching composing.

   A teacher's ed. for the author's textbook: Composing:
writing as a self-creating process.
   1. English language—Rhetoric—Study and teaching.
I. Title.
PE1404.C6   808′.04275   74-10989
ISBN 0-8104-5840-3
ISBN 0-8104-5839-X (pbk.)

Copyright © 1974 by HAYDEN BOOK COMPANY, INC. All rights reserved.
No part of this book may be reprinted, or reproduced, or utilized in any
form or by any electronic, mechanical, or other means, now known or
hereafter invented, including photocopying and recording, or in any information storage and retrieval system, without permission in writing from
the Publisher.

Printed in the United States of America

        1   2   3   4   5   6   7   8   9   PRINTING

      74 75 76 77 78 79 80 81 82   YEAR

Preface

This book has been compiled and arranged to serve two purposes. For teachers of writing who are working with the textbook *Composing: Writing as a Self-Creating Process*—a text included here as the section entitled "To the Student" and the thirty assignments themselves—it is intended as a teacher's manual. For teachers or prospective teachers of English, or anyone else with an interest in the subject of composition generally, the book is a description of a way of offering students an opportunity to increase their ability with the English language by increasing their consciousness of the ways in which their lives are composed by language, and vice versa.

For neither group of readers do I intend the approach and discussion to be seen as in any way prescriptive. My comments on the genesis of the assignments, the nature and shape of the course in which they were used, and the ways in which I see each of them individually and sequentially as involving students with problems of language, I offer as no more than a way of providing other teachers with what I as a teacher of writing try to make available to students: a style performed in such a way as to enable someone else to make, or to make better, a style of his own. Thus, although I am concerned in this book with describing a way of introducing students to seeing *writing* as a creative process, as an activity of making or building construed as an activity of moment and worth, I am just as concerned with the *teaching of writing* as an activity to be seen in exactly the same terms. It is in this sense that the ambiguity of the title is intended—and that I would have my procedure understood.

William E. Coles, Jr.

Acknowledgments

For Assignment 28, for the idea for the assignments on rote learning, and for the passages quoted in Assignments 6 and 18, I am indebted to Professor Theodore Baird of Amherst College.

For the diagram of the Perfect Student, and for the idea for Assignments 1 and 7, I am indebted to Professor John F. Butler of George Peabody College for Teachers.

Contents

TEACHING COMPOSING

To the Teacher

The Course and the Assignments: Background

Perhaps the best introduction to the assignments in this book is to explain how they came about and what those of us who have worked with them had in mind as their purpose.

We started, the four of us * who put together the pilot course for the staff-taught writing program at Drexel University, with the shared understanding that, although no one can make someone else a writer, it was possible to do better than pretend that we did not believe this, or to behave as though we wished it were not true. To put our course together we began with the assumption that since the process of writing as a process is as important for what it is about as for what it is, then the real value of a course in writing may be said to lie beyond that activity in something else. We assumed, that is, that we would be giving our students the most that we could give them, not by asking them to become writers, not even by asking them to imagine what they could do if they were writers, but by putting them into a position to see what they could learn about language and themselves as language-users through their attempts to act like writers. We wanted a course in writing that would be a course in language as well, a course that would have as its subject the activity of *composing* in the largest possible sense of the term. We wanted a course that would enable us to suggest to students the ways in which their lives, no less than their papers, are composed, composed by language, designed and arranged by the symbol systems through which all of us see the world and by which we are in turn given the identities we have. We intended, therefore, to develop a course that would deal with the workings of English in such a way as to demonstrate how an understanding of one language was relevant to an understanding of language in general—a procedure that we hoped would give, say, a future mathematician at least the opportunity through his experience with writing English to become more aware of himself as a user of the language of mathematics.

The first step that we took in translating our assumptions into a syllabus and a procedure was in a sense a step to the side, a step to eliminate the more obvious guarantees of our seeing our students' writing as something other than writing, of our seeing writing as other than a matter of the workings of language. We did not want to develop a course that would

* I would like here to express my gratitude to my colleagues, Professors Robert Holland, Miriam Kotzin, and Murray Miller, for helping make that staff course an education in itself.

require some special knowledge or training either to take or to teach—a course in linguistics, for example, or the philosophy of language. Nor did we want to ground our course in the notion that our students had to be painstakingly taught the rudiments of English usage—not because some of them do not need such instruction, but because we believed (and still do) that at a university the responsibility to write decently belongs to the student alone; and we found that the enactment of this belief in the form of a refusal to deal with indecency was the fastest way to obtain the standards we behaved as though we were simply taking for granted. Neither did we want our course to have as its subject some focus to which the act of the student's composing his own experience in words, sentences, paragraphs was subsidiary. So we decided to get rid of everything that teachers and students alike are tempted to look at writing from behind or through or under. The anthology went; so did the standard plays, novels, and poems. We threw out the style manual, even the handbook. Above all the handbook. We left ourselves as we left our students with no more than the assignments of this text to make a course of, a common body of materials that each of us used to run his own class his own way. For all of us, like it or not, the subject was going to be writing as language, for that was all we had left: our assignments and class exercises, the students' papers, and each other.

The nominal subject we used as a way of asking our students to become conscious of themselves as writers was that of teaching and learning: What does it mean to teach or to be taught? How does one go about learning? What is the function of language in these processes? How does one make use of his way of addressing such questions in order to locate himself as a language user in relation to his own education? We did not want to dump on our students a mere potpourri of problems relating to teaching and learning any more than we wanted to create a programmed text, a set of assignments marching syllogistically to some predetermined Grand Conclusion. We wanted a syllabus that would have to be arranged into some sort of pattern—a pattern which for better or worse in being the expression of what each individual had made his experience with the course mean to him would also be the expression of each individual's understanding of himself as a language user.

Before we began the term I devised a set of problems intended to involve us in a consideration of these questions from a number of different perspectives, a sort of ur-syllabus that gave us at least a place to begin, a tentative way for the course to proceed, and somewhere for us to come out. I designed each problem, one for every class meeting of the term, so that it could be used as either a class exercise or a writing assignment. "Problem" here is perhaps a misleading word, at least to the extent that it implies providing the students with an intellectual jigsaw puzzle to fit together—some carefully disassembled construct to which every piece was equally relevant and all the pieces relevant in only a certain way. What I tried to bring together in each assignment was a set of propositions and questions that would have to be formulated into a problem, that each student would have to shape into a problem that he would then go on to address. For this reason, most of the assignments contained (and still do) a great deal of information and a great many questions that could be dealt with in a number of different ways. How a student put these materials together, what he chose to deal with or to ignore in the questions asked of him, what form his paper was to take—all of this was to be left to him.

As a staff we met once a week to consider each of the items of the syllabus we were planning to use the following week—scrapping, substituting, rewriting, rearranging until we had the wording of each item and the order of things in a form acceptable to all of us. This was an exacting as well as an exciting procedure, our way of making sure, first of all, that we would communicate with one another (in much the same way that we were demanding our students communicate with us). Our object was to make what we were teaching in common represent the very best that our pooled intellectual resources were capable of creating. Secondly, we wanted to stay as pure as we could in what we were doing, to keep our questions open in such a way as to allow each of us, four very different kinds of teachers, to preserve and refine the integrity of his own style.

In form and arrangement, then, the assignments of the text represent the consensus of four teachers who worked with them. They have already been revised, many of them more than once, on the basis of our classroom experiences with them, and we are confident that any teacher anywhere can use them as the basis for a course in composition just as they are written and with every expectation of educational success. On the other hand, this does not mean that the form the assignments have ought to be considered canonical. Other teachers, working either in groups or by themselves, may well decide to revise the assignments further. Some teachers, for example, may on certain assignments consider certain clusterings of questions irrelevant to their purposes and simply cut them. Other teachers may have their students focus on a single question or a single set of questions rather than on the assignment as a totality. It is possible with certain assignments to use supplementary readings. And, of course, there may be assignments here that some teachers may not wish to use at all.

Finally, no matter how the text is used, each teacher is going to have to adapt it on the basis of how many papers he decides he is going to have his students write and also of which assignments he is going to have them address these papers to. As is noted in the introduction to the student, since the assignments exist to make possible a number of different ways of talking about what they are about, there is no one way to use them, nothing in them that cannot be rearranged, rephrased, added to, or deleted as the style of a teacher, the length of a term, the requirements of a course, or the level of a class determines. And for the same reason, the same assignments may be used by the same teacher—or the same group of teachers—again and again.

The Course and the Assignments: General Comments

From here on I will speak as I did in my memoranda to our first staff, as though I were addressing a group of colleagues interested in working together to teach a course in writing. My responsibility as the creator of the assignments is to be of what help I can in explaining my intentions and expectations. The following notes are to be considered as no more than an attempt to start a conversation or a line of thinking, and my pronouncements are to be understood as representing only my notion of a procedure for myself. This is the only purpose of my comments, and it is worth repeating that they cannot be of any help to anyone if seen as any more than the enactment of the style of an individual teacher against which other teachers must define themselves. I'd like first to speak on the course and the assignments in general and then address myself to the assignments one by one.

*　　*　　*

Let us be clear at the outset that there are certain risks to what we are doing, and that we will not in eleven weeks—or more or less—either as individuals or as a group be able to perform a miracle. Inside that outside limit, however, there seems to me a lot that we *can* do, a lot we can become interested in ourselves and learn from each other (and from our students) about the mysterious matter of what it means to write a sentence in English.

I feel a great openness about what we can do together this term. It is true that to put thirty assignments, as well as a general introduction to the student, before you all at once is to suggest that everything has been planned and arranged in advance. But please do not take every word in every assignment too seriously. This planning is just the best I can do during the summer, a way of giving us something to rearrange or to find substitutes for, a place to start. The problems I have constructed for the term represent no more than one more try at the forever fascinating question of how anyone teaches anyone else anything. And so far as answers to the questions are concerned, all I profess is a readiness to go looking for them; all I expect is to be able to frame an answer according to a given situation. Every assignment, every question, every problem presents new possibilities—if it is any good to begin with.

What I aim at in an assignment is the creation of the possibility where a student may say something he has not said before, where he has the chance to find himself in the act of expression, the chance to become conscious of himself as a writer, a user of language or languages. It really doesn't matter very much what an assignment is about so long as it seems in phase with where a set of assignments is headed and so long as it seems to offer possibilities for a writer (and has interest for a teacher) by posing an open question.

When it comes to the teaching of writing, I have my bias and you have yours, but I think generally that we want the same things of ourselves and of our students, that we share more than we differ on. And to keep in mind what we do share is to cause our differences to become interesting, to enable an articulation of them to give us a chance to grow as teachers. So I am not deeply troubled by the thought that my suggestions for the term are also a reflection of how I look at things, what I have been taught and taught myself to do in the classroom. It is precisely what we have the right to expect of each other.

Let me say what I think we do share. This is a writing course we will be teaching together, a course that has writing, and not something else, as its subject. Our aim as teachers is to involve the student in his own writing, to engage his interest as much as possible in his own writing, and then to tell him whatever we can about what he has said and how he has said it. We do this not simply to increase our students' verbal sophistication as readers and writers, but because we believe that what the. activities of reading and writing are concerned with, the use of language to locate one's self at a given moment in time, can have something to do with who one chooses to become, maybe even with who he chooses to be. We would have students know something of the function of language, then, because we would have them aware that they cannot live on any level other than that of the languages with which they are able to function. We would have students able to determine the shapes of their lives rather than live lives which have been determined for them. We would like to see students masters of language, not slaves to it. No doubt you have your own favorite phrasing of High Sounding Purpose. I hope that along with having to cope with our day by day situation as teachers this term we will be talking occasionally about how to improve our understanding and our expression of what we are up to when we teach composition.

But on a more worldly level.

The metaphor, the nominal subject I am proposing we use to help the students become conscious of themselves as users of language, is that of teaching and learning. Although the assignments themselves provide the best statement I know how to make of the "progression" of the course—what it is we start with, where it is we come out—perhaps it may be of help for me to explain in general terms how I move from Assignment 1 to Assignment 30. After the first two assignments—an overview of the relation of teaching and learning to language—the chronology of the course begins by having the student examine some commonplaces about learning (Assignments 3 through 6), some of the simple (and often simple-minded) ways in which the learning process is represented as both understandable and understood by everybody. I do this in order to invite the students to confront the distance between what is likely to be their conventional expression of some equally conventional assumptions about the learning process, and the complexity, the mysteriousness of the act of learning itself. Or, in terms of our real subject, what I wish to dramatize for students in the first two weeks of the course is the distance between the ways they have been taught (and have taught themselves) to write and to see, and the nature of their experience as they live and feel it. (The students' attitudes toward rote learning, for example, I'm pretty sure will emerge as disparaging—and as rote-learned.)

I then invite the students to make some connections between the act of learning and the use of language: first, by asking them to consider some of the implications of an act of learning seen as an action with language (Assignment 7)—a process in which the quality of one would seem to depend on the quality of the other (Assignments 8 through 10) —and second, by asking them to examine the relation of approach to result in the context of some specific examples of the learning process (Assignments 11 through 17). Assignments 18 to 20, which have to do with teachers and responses to teaching, are for the purpose of developing another perspective from which to see the relationship of language to the learning process, a perspective that Assignments 21 through 23 ask that the students take into account through a reexamination of their assumptions about what it means to be a student. In the assignments leading to the final paper (24 through 29), I ask the students to confront the question of what barriers there are to learning and to explore the ambiguity of attitude with which all of us regard the process of education when it is seen in terms of a change of self. The final assignment is an attempt to bring things full circle by asking the students to declare themselves on the importance language has in their lives—in terms, I hope, which will make clear that our demand is for an individual writer's conclusions for himself, not a demand for the regurgitation of some non-existent party line.

The syllabus I've worked out has the students writing somewhere between twelve and fourteen papers for the course, but this number is tentative and can easily be increased or decreased because of the nature of the syllabus. I've put together each of the problems in such a way as to make it possible to use any one of them as either a writing assignment or an assignment for class discussion.

*   *   *

General Introduction

The introductory description of the course addressed to the student is not only for the purpose of letting a student know what he is in for, but also for the purpose of defining the relation of the student to his education, the student to his teacher, the student and the teacher to their subject. For until we can think clearly of what all of us are doing in the classroom, misunderstanding and dissatisfaction are inevitable. I do not say, you will notice, that the statement will eliminate all future misunderstanding and dissatisfaction. Indeed, to judge from my experience with such statements in the past, I have little hope that many students will understand how much we are trying to say to them in it—not because the statement is difficult to understand, but because it is difficult for students to believe. Most students, even when they are being dealt with honestly by English teachers, have trouble imagining that they can afford the luxury of believing them. "No doctrine to the assignments is there? Nothing for a student to become aware of and give back to a teacher? There's no formula here I'm going to be able to discover and make use of? I mean, man, says who?" Most of this goes on at a semiconscious level to be sure, but it is a given of an English teacher's situation and you know the reasons for it as well as I do.

The best we can do with this situation is to be as straight as possible about what we are doing in a statement that students will understand more fully as the term goes on, a statement that can grow in meaning to them as they grow with our procedures and our subject. I will spend the first class meeting reading it over aloud with the students, editorializing where I think it will help, answering questions, and laying the ground rules by which my sections will be run. I'll want my students to know, for example, that when I use mimeographed samples of their writing to talk about in class I won't use names. I'll want them to know also that they may rewrite as many times as they wish any paper they are disappointed in, that this is a standing invitation, and that I will read as many versions of as many papers as they have energy to produce. I'll explain my policy of taking literacy for granted (and mention the availability of handbooks in the bookstore for those who think they might need one). And I'll want them to know that whereas I will keep a record of their work, grades will not be placed on individual papers. Finally, I'll tell them what I can about the way we'll proceed with the assignments as a class: that we'll take them (or their equivalents) one by one, but that since it's not an Easter egg hunt we're on, it doesn't matter whether they read ahead if they want to; that we may be making substitutions or changes in the wording and order of the assignments; that they'll be writing somewhere between ten and fifteen papers; and so on.

I think we say everything that should be said to the students in the introductory description about how to handle the writing assignments, so I don't intend to tell them not to take up the questions of an assignment mechanically or that they should plan to deal only with what seem to them to be the key questions, the most important issues of an assignment. How a writer chooses to handle an assignment, after all, is part of what he has to say about it. Mechanical approaches to the assignments or instances of evasiveness (matters of problem formulation, really) I'd rather handle after the fact and as a matter of choice in terms of an individual student's paper. Of course I am speaking now only of *my* pedagogical style. I can easily see how another teacher might want to say something this first period about what he expects a student to do when he writes a paper.

So far as practical matters are concerned, I'll have my students buy a notebook to hold both the papers they've written as well as the sample papers we'll be working with, and I'll have them bring this notebook together with the text to class regularly. I'll conclude things by telling the students to come to class next time prepared to write.

To the Student

The assignments of this text are designed to be used for a course in writing, a course in which writing, specifically your writing, is the center. Their aim is to offer you an opportunity to become a better reader and writer, first by giving you a meaningful subject to read and write about, and second, by making it possible for you to use your attempts to improve yourself as a reader and a writer to learn something about language and yourself as a language user: what language is, how it functions, why it is important. In practice you will find that these two aims become reflexes of each other. To become more knowledgeable about language is to increase your ability to manipulate it, just as to become a better reader and writer is to enlarge your understanding of the nature of language and its significance in your life. One learns to read and write by reading and writing—and by taking seriously, because he understands the importance of taking seriously, what it is he is doing.

The nominal subject of the assignments is teaching and learning. This subject provides you with something relevant to your immediate experience to think and write about, and serves also to give class conversation a focus, the day by day movement of a course some kind of shape and direction. But the real subject of the assignments is language, and their real function is to involve you with the activity of language using, of *composing* in the largest sense of the word. They are constructed to give you the chance to work out in your own terms and for yourself what it means to see yourself as a composer of your own reality. For composed this reality is, composed by language, or more accurately by languages, those various arrangements of terminologies or names or symbols (whatever you may wish to call them) with which each one of us frames and organizes the world he lives in and by which, for better or for worse, each one of us is framed and organized.

The idea behind this way of seeing writing is that you will have a better chance to write better sentences if you have some idea of what a sentence is, and of what it can mean to write one, than if you don't. For simply to write sentences, all of them for someone else, with no consciousness of what the activity can involve or of how it can be important, is as meaningless as it is boring; and it is hard to imagine how anyone for whom the activity of writing is no more than this could care very much about writing at all, let alone whether he gets any better at it. But to understand the activity of writing in such a way as to develop a consciousness of oneself as a manipulator of language and of his experience as arranged, defined, and evaluated by the languages which shape it, is to have the chance to discover also the ways in which one's identity as a person is dependent upon the languages he commands. This consciousness, which the assignments are contrived in a variety of ways to move you toward, will not automatically make you a writer, but it can provide you with the chance to understand the activity of writing as an activity with meaning—as important for what it is *about* as for what it is. It can provide you with the chance to understand, in whatever language you work with, at least the significance of creating a voice of your own.

These assignments, then, are intended for a course in writing that is a course in language as well: a course in composing, selecting and arranging, putting together. The medium of communication you will be working with is largely the English language—largely though not entirely, for in addressing some assignments you may wish to use colored pencils and crayons to make sketches; or perhaps you may choose to express relationships in mathematical notation or with equations. And even though it is with experience expressed in terms of words, sentences, paragraphs, with the workings of the English langauge, that most of the assignments concern themselves, these operations are looked at in such a way as to invite you to understand them as common to the workings of language in general—whether that language is made up of mathematical or chemical symbols, shapes and colors on canvas, gestures, or words. The assignments, in other words, seek to make it possible for a future physicist, say, through his attempts to improve himself in English, to become more responsible to himself as a user of the language of physics.

The emphasis here, you will notice, falls heavily on the notion of invitation, on the assignments as offering you a chance or an opportunity. This is deliberate and is intended as a compliment. In certain courses, and at certain levels of education, the substance of knowledge—what the participants in the process are to think about—is supplied by the teacher or the textbook; the term paper, the quiz, and the examination then serve to measure how much has been retained by the student of what has been transmitted to him. But with these assignments nothing is transmitted to you, nothing is demanded of you in this way. In order to deal with them you will be supplying your own information and material. After all, you have held various jobs and played games. You live in a variety of communities. And for a number of years now you have had your own thoughts and feelings about things. This is your experience, and from this seemingly shapeless and yet entirely individual source you will derive whatever it is you have to say. In this sense, all of the questions of all of the assignments may be understood to involve the same issues: where and how with this problem do you locate your self? To what extent and in what ways is this self definable in language? What is this self on the basis of the language shaping it here? What has it got to do with you?

You should understand that the self being spoken of above, and the one that you will be concerned with in the classroom, is a literary self; not a mock or false self, but a stylistic self, the self construable from the

way words fall in a conversation or on a page. The other self, your identity as a person, is something that no teacher as a teacher can have very
much to do with. That there is a relation between these two selves, between writing and thinking, intellect and being, a very complicated and
involving relation indeed—this is undeniable. This relation, in fact, is the
center of both the assignments as assignments and the assignments as
more than that. But the nature of this relation, that of the self to the roles
or styles in which it finds expression and through which it grows, is one
that only an individual writer or thinker has the right to work out, and it
can hardly become the province of public discourse without a teacher's
ceasing to be a teacher, a student's ceasing to be a student. Ideally, hopefully, primarily, the concern of the assignments is with words; not with
thinking, but with a language about thinking; not with people or selves,
but with languages about people and selves. If your teacher seems to refuse, therefore, either to sympathize with or to condemn a self outside
the words it has chosen to have shape, it is because he believes that you
are a person as well as a student, that you have a life as well as roles,
and a life that no one has the right to interfere with. Few teachers are
either equipped for or ready to assume the responsibility of posing as
parents, priests, or psychoanalysts.

While you supply the material for your own discourse, the assignments are contrived both to direct a general movement from day to day
throughout the term and to enable you to move from their nominal subject to their real one. In this sense the assignments have a chronology.
They are arranged. The first few assignments, for example, ask you to
isolate a bit of your experience and then ask you something about what
you have done in this act of separating one thing from another, of arranging what you know in some sort of pattern. Subsequent assignments provide you with additional perspectives from which to question this pattern,
to widen or narrow or otherwise revise it if you want to. How you put
together the materials given you to work with in an assignment, what you
choose to deal with and what you choose to ignore in the questions asked
of you, what form you will give to the papers you write—these are matters
that most of the time will be left strictly up to you. That is, the problems
you will be addressing will be up to you in a certain sense to formulate.
As you move from assignment to assignment you will be making increasingly complicated statements about yourself as a writer, a composer,
a language user—statements which you will be asked finally to take into
consideration in making some sort of order out of your experience with
the assignments as a whole, some sort of sense of where you started with
them and of where you seem to come out.

It must be emphatically said that the assignments themselves are not
an argument. They contain no doctrine, either individually or as a sequence. There is no philosophy in them, either homespun or highflown, for
a teacher to become aware of and give to students, for students to become

aware of and give back to a teacher. Above all, the questions of the assignments must be understood as invariably open, as questions to be addressed rather than answered. In fact, the assignments are arranged and phrased precisely to make impossible the discovery in them of anything like a master plan. They are put together in such a way as to mean only and no more than what the various responses they are constructed to evoke can be made to mean, a meaning that will be different for different teachers and students as well as differently come by. In a paper addressed, for example, to Assignment 15, a student may work out a connection with a paper that he (or someone else) wrote for Assignment 7, which at Assignment 20, after a discussion of Assignment 19, may be the subject of a paper in which he changes his interpretation of the problem of Assignment 5. Other students may move in other ways.

Thus, at the same time that the creation of some pattern for your experience with the assignments will be necessary if you are to make anything of them at all, an infinite number of patterns for them is possible. This is not to say, of course, that every pattern, every way of addressing a question, is as good as every other, but it is to say that whatever continuity you construct from assignment to assignment, from one paper to another, from one class discussion to the next, is your continuity and yours alone. It is this continuity, this meaning, which in expressing your understanding of yourself as a language user will express also what you make your experience with the subject of composing mean to you. Whatever you learn from your experience with these assignments, you learn. Whatever you make of your awareness of the activity of writing as an activity of language is up to you.

Since the assignments exist to make possible a number of different ways of talking about what they are about, there is no one way to use them, nothing in them that cannot be rearranged, rephrased, added to, or deleted as the style of a teacher, the length of a term, the requirements of a course, or the character of a class determines. Your teacher may have you focus on a single aspect of an assignment, for example, rather than work with it as a totality. Or you may be asked to work with passages other than or in addition to those provided by the text. Perhaps your teacher will alter the order of the assignments or construct some of his own to replace or supplement what is here. And because each assignment is designed to be used as either a writing assignment or a class exercise, something to talk through in discussion, it will have to be decided how many papers you are going to write and which assignments you will address these papers to. This text, in other words, is not itself a composition course. It merely provides the materials for one.

Your teacher will read your papers, comment on them, and bring examples of your writing to class to talk about. In your attempts to improve yourself as a writer, to enlarge your understanding of the nature and function of language in your life, he will be of what help to you he can. But do not expect him to tell you how to proceed with an assignment, how to find something in your experience to talk about, or how to make a given issue relevant or meaningful in terms of your own life. No one can do this for another. For the same reason it is unreal to expect that your teacher will be able to tell you how to improve your writing. If anyone could tell someone else how to do this, then courses in writing would not be necessary. The best a teacher can do, a course can do, an education can do, is to put you in a position to improve yourself for yourself—and be ready to acknowledge your effort.

1. Teaching and Learning: Expectations

In order to write papers for a course in writing, you must make a start somewhere. Our subject is language, but the metaphor we will be using in order to try to understand a little of how we use words, how we define words and make sense, is the process of teaching and learning. The assignments, then, are a means of starting a conversation about our subject, starting it and keeping it going. If you consider each paper you write as something less than a final pronouncement, less the means of closing a question than of keeping it open, you will put yourself in a position to learn more.

* * *

This writing assignment is for the purpose of sorting you out as individuals. Your paper will be read as soon as you have written it, but will not be returned to you until later in the term.

(Have your English teachers in the past always returned your work to you right away? Do you find yourself at all suspicious of the claim that "your paper will be read as soon as you have written it"?)

Although most of your experience with formal education has been required of you by law, you are now at the stage of having a choice of whether to continue with it or not. This means that you have certainly speculated, however remotely, on why you are now attending an educational institution instead of doing something else, on what it is you imagine you are doing here, on the meaning of a formal education in the context of your own life.

Address yourself to what you expect of the process of teaching and learning in the time you will spend here. What is it you want to learn exactly? How do you propose to go about doing it? Do you intend to do as you're told, is that what learning consists of? Or do you intend to do something other than what you're told? Is there anything you would like to learn in your formal education that you doubt you can? And what do you expect of your teachers? Are they to provide information only? Are they to interfere with your way of thinking? Do you have an idea of what a Good Teacher is? What's a Good Student?

If you find it difficult to draw lines here, face your puzzlement squarely. What is it that you find baffling or perplexing about such a subject? It is, after all, your education you're talking about.

Commentary

I suggest we use Assignment 1 as an in-class writing assignment (though you can have them do it out of class if you'd like to; it won't make any difference in terms of result). It is, as you can see, a kind of shotgun approach to the whole issue of teaching and learning. The parenthesized paragraph is for the purpose of at least nudging the students into wondering whether the sort of stock talk they're so used to producing for English courses is going to be appropriate for this one. This is also the reason for the capitalizations and for the whole final paragraph. I've done what I can in that paragraph (and in my phrasing of the questions of the next to last paragraph also) to suggest that there are real problems for real people to this issue, to seek to make possible what I don't expect we'll get very much of: an honest confession of mystification, a human voice speaking its humanness. What I do expect we'll get, what I'm pretty sure we'd get with any opening writing assignment, is Themewriting. Cant.

I don't think that the students are going to see very much in this issue to be puzzled about, not any more than I expect that their papers are going to enable us to sort them out as individuals—and for exactly the same reason. Unless students this term are different from what they have been for centuries, we are not going to be addressed by individuals at all. What we will hear from is the Perfect Student, Mr. Corporate Identity, who will inform us that he has come to college to be Educated: to be guided, steered, directed, formed, shaped, molded, and so on by Teachers, whose sympathy, understanding, tolerance, and unfailing goodwill he can depend upon to throw the switch that will painlessly complete the circuit of knowledge (though we will also be told, with no sense of the contradiction involved, of the necessity for the "digestion" or "incorporation" of this Knowledge and of the vital importance of everyone's learning to Think For Himself). There will be some variation in the papers, I suppose, but not enough to make that much difference. I plan to verify this on the basis of a quick reading, but I won't mark this set of papers (that will be up to the students to do for themselves on Assignment 30). Just before I give the papers back at the end of the term, I'll read through them quickly again, in order to be able to write no more than a single question at the end of each one.

Before the students begin writing Assignment 1 in class, I'll make two assignments. I'll ask them to have prepared both Assignments 2 and 3 by our next class meeting. Assignment 3 I'll ask them to address with a paper (which we'll take up in class the period after they turn it in). Assignment 2 (which we'll talk about at our next, our second, class meeting) I'll have them prepare as a class exercise. I'll also tell them to write out some notes on the questions of Assignment 2 and to bring them to class to talk from.

2. Holding Hands

Before a large public audience, a Famous Man recently started a speech by saying:

Holding hands is not really so easy a thing to do as many people think. How to hold hands is something a person must learn.

This statement was greeted with long applause by all elements of the audience. Without knowing more than what you are told here about those elements, speculate on why the speaker was applauded. To do this, consider the following information and questions.

1. In the audience was a group of young people, aged 17 to 21 (mostly college students), many of whom would be called "hippies" by older people. A number of these people applauded vigorously, some of them looking with scorn at the over-40 members of the audience. What do you suppose these applauding young people took the speaker's statement to mean?

2. Why do you suppose that a number of them looked with scorn at the over-40s?

3. Many of the over-40s also applauded. The speaker himself was over 50. What do you suppose these applauding over-40s took the speaker to mean?

4. Some of the applauding over-40s sneered back at the young people, as if in triumph. What do you suppose they thought their triumph consisted of?

5. Also in the audience was a small group of people who were in the middle of a week-long Sensitivity Training Workshop. They *stood* and applauded, but instead of sneering at others, they looked as if they felt pity for them. What do you suppose this group took the speaker to mean?

6. Why do you suppose they looked with pity on the others?

7. To judge from the speaker's sentences quoted at the beginning of this exercise, can *you* tell what he means?

8. Do you see any way that the people in the audience could tell what the speaker meant any better than you can?

9. Then how do you account for such different groups of people with such (presumably) different sets of values behaving as they did?

10. Now, back to our story. Upon hearing the applause of the audience, the Famous Man quoted above stopped, smiled, and then simply sat down. At that point, all elements of the audience applauded even more enthusiastically. What do you suppose the various elements of the audience took the speaker's smiling and sitting down to mean?

11. What do you think the speaker's smiling and sitting down might have meant?

12. The speaker used language, or more accurately languages. To interpret him, the audience also used language. From this point of view, what does the phenomenon you have been considering here enable you to conclude about the nature and function of language?

13. Can you conclude anything about the importance of language to teaching? To learning?

Commentary

I'll begin class by collecting the papers addressed to Assignment 3 (which I'll tell the students, again, that we'll consider at our next class meeting through mimeographed samples of their writing), and also have them write a paper addressing Assignment 4 to hand in at that same next meeting. The Wordsworth section of Assignment 4, I'll explain, is on the same problem that they are to concern themselves with in their papers, and they are to make of it what they can. Their papers, however, are to address only the section of the assignment following the asterisks.

*   *   *

"Holding Hands" fills an hour instructively and the students generally seem to enjoy talking about it. Whereas there are a number of directions in which we can move with the exercise, I plan to use it with my classes to dramatize three things in particular: to make clear first of all that language is more than a matter of words (hence the questions on the speaker's smiling and sitting down); secondly, to suggest that an interpretation of language is also a matter of language—that what in this instance is heard or experienced is what the various elements of the audience have told themselves they have heard and experienced; and finally to show how a clichéd use of language (the stereotypes with which all elements of the audience seem to be thinking) can turn the world and one's self into less than they are.

There is, as I see it, no way of telling what the speaker might have meant by what he said or by smiling and sitting down, but the fun of the exercise in class will be to deal with speculation after speculation in order to make clear to the students that that is what they are—

possible meanings that no one can make into anything more than possibilities without becoming in effect as blind as one of the groups of the audience. I plan also in this connection to invite the students to decide which group is most blind (it's the people of the sensitivity session I think), as a way of introducing them to the notion of certainty as a barrier to learning. I will count my class successful if with the last two questions I can do no more than open the students' awareness to language as a concept, as having something to do with what it means to hear and see and think as well as with the act of expression (and in this sense as having something to do with teaching and learning as processes). That language is both the basis of, and at the same time the largest obstacle to, the activities of teaching and learning I hope will be an implicit formulation of our discussion, but I don't expect the paradox will mean very much to the students at this point even if I should get a chance to state it.

3. *Really Knowing*

Here is what a teacher of writing has to say of the papers he wrote as a student for an English course in college:

> . . . My own papers in that course were generally regurgitated liberalism. . . . There was nothing in them that came from my own experience, my own notions of what would constitute evidence for my conclusions. There I was, in Utah in the depths of the depression, writing about the Okies when I could have been writing about the impoverished farmers all around me. I wrote about race relations in the South without ever having talked with a Negro in my life and without recognizing that the bootblack I occasionally saw in Salt Lake City in the Hotel Utah was in any way related to the problem of race relations. . . . My life, my observations, my insights were not included in those papers on the Okies and race relations and the New Deal. Every opinion was derivative, every observation second-hand. . . . What I wrote was therefore characterless, without true personality, though often full of personal pronouns.
>
> *—Wayne Booth* *

An obvious conclusion to be drawn from Booth's evaluation of his work is that he was not writing about his own experience, about what he really knew of the world around him. (And why not, do you imagine? Did he have a Bad English Teacher? A Poor Background? Was he just Lazy? Any other possibilities?) It is no surprise, therefore, to find him advising teachers of writing to get their students "to write about something they know about."

> Papers about ideas written by sheep are boring; papers written by thinking boys and girls are interesting. The problem is always to find ideas at a level that will allow the student to reason, that is, to provide support for his ideas, rather than merely assert them in half-baked form. And this means something that is all too often forgotten by the most ambitious teachers—namely, that whatever ideas the student writes about must somehow be connected with his own experience.*

* Excerpts from "Boring from Within: The Art of the Freshman Essay," by Wayne C. Booth are reprinted from *The Norton Reader,* third edition, Arthur M. Eastman, Gen. Ed. By permission of W. W. Norton & Company, Inc. Copyright © 1973, 1969, 1965 by W. W. Norton & Company, Inc.

If you were to apply these remarks to your own activity as a writer, what would you say you really "know about"? What "ideas" would you point to as being "connected with [your] own experience"? How would you talk about them?

Choose such an idea, something you feel you really "know about," and write a paper in which you make clear exactly how the idea is connected with your life as you are living it.

On the basis of what you have written, can you see any reason for your having pointed where you have?

Commentary

Again, I'll begin class by collecting the papers addressed to Assignment 4 and have the students write a paper addressing Assignment 5 to be turned in at the next class meeting.

*   *   *

This will be our first class meeting on the students' writing, and though I would like to be proved wrong, what I think we're going to have to deal with is what we have to deal with in any set of papers addressed to any first assignment with any group of students in a writing course— no matter what level our students were on, or what the subject was, or how we offered it. I don't think, in other words, that the distinctions made in the quotations from Booth are going to make any difference in what the students will do on their papers. (In fact, I've chosen the passages that I have precisely to make clear the distinction between knowing what to do as a writer and being able to do it.) "What 'ideas' would you point to . . . how would you talk about them" I imagine will be interpreted to mean: "Where do you point when you're writing English papers for an English Teacher; how do you talk when you think you're being asked to display your credentials?" The majority of students, therefore, will be writing trumpery, clichés: on the equality of all men; the awfulness of pollution, corruption of various sorts, and war; the necessity for decency and clear communication in human relations; and so on. I'm not suggesting that the students will simply write out a string of abstractions they don't believe in. I'm suggesting that very few of them will write on what is important to them in the *way* that it is important to them. What they will "point to" (without being aware of it) is an area of language, a word bin filled with prefabricated phraseology, a vocabulary at one with a syntax. "Your life as you are living it" I don't expect to be much in the running.

In short, I think that what we will be dealing with on this assignment is deadness, phoniness, what Ken Macrorie (in *Uptaught*) calls Engfish and what we are calling Themewriting. I think we will get a great many papers with something like this as their paradigm:

Singling out some aspect of "knowledge knitted into our very being" is difficult. Having knowledge in a wide variety of areas makes it difficult to point out an area, topic or idea that I know well. I have greater knowledge in some areas than others however, and I feel that ———— is my stronger subject. I realize that my knowledge is limited, but for my years of schooling I believe that I can talk intelligently about matters of ————. ———— particularly is an area that I want to learn as much about as I can and hope to retain everything I have learned. The knowledge I now have is permanent, and will not dwindle away through years of disuse. Hopefully I will use my knowledge often and it will service myself as well as others.

I do not believe in the idea that great knowledge is yours alone, that you cannot really communicate knowledge to someone else. For if you have knowledge and share it with someone, then no one has lost anything, everyone has gained. To me, gaining knowledge and helping people are what life is all about. That is why I really have no desire to be anything but a teacher. The field I have chosen is inhuman enough, without sitting at a machine or not working with people.

The entire idea of having "knowledge knitted into your very being" conveys the message of having knowledge, using it, and keeping it forever.

Man doesn't just know things. By this I mean that man isn't a machine that just memorizes facts. He can think, he has feelings, and he can make decisions. These are the things that make man a true human being. Even in our advanced society today many people walk around acting like machines. They become this way because of some of the ways that they make their living. Working in a factory, on an assembly line, doing the same thing over and over requires no thinking and no great skill. This is a great shame that people have to live like this.

As a student it would be very easy to become like a machine since you are always being fed information. But on the other hand a student also has to think and use his imagination. Writing is a good example of this. The knowledge that a student is acquiring will become useful later in his life when he is finally in the position to use his vast resources of knowledge to create.

That, by the way, is a real student paper and not something I just made up for the occasion. It was addressed to an assignment very much like the one we are using (the metaphor for "really 'know about' " in the earlier assignment was "something knitted into your very being"). Could you guess, could anyone possibly, that the terms I have replaced with blanks above were "science" (in the one case "physical science")? Could you tell from the paper as the student has written it that he too was asked to make some connection between this knowledge that is "knitted into [his] very being" and his life as he is living it, and that he was asked also to account for how it was he had written his paper as he had? This is what I mean by suggesting that the distinctions we set up for the students with our directives in this paper are not going to make much difference in what they do (though I think it tremendously important for us to have them there to refer to—and to refer back to).

In this set of papers I expect students to sound the way they think they ought to sound, the way they think we want them to sound, the way they think they have been taught to sound. Whatever we give them they will bend in that direction. Whatever attempts we make to head them off they will have a tendency to ignore. And our students will do this not because they have been badly taught or because they have no moral character (the reason for the parenthetical queries in the assignment), but simply because it is tremendously difficult to see for one's self and in one's own terms. In other words, we are not setting a trap for the students with this assignment, as I see it, so much as we are setting up an assignment to invite them to examine the trap they have put themselves in. We are inviting them to see how they sound when they believe that they know what is going to be expected of them. (This, incidentally, is what I think went wrong with Booth's papers in that course he speaks of; I don't believe he would have written his papers much differently, not at the start, even if his teacher *had* specified that he deal with those "impoverished farmers" or that bootblack in the Hotel Utah. It wasn't Booth's subject that was wrong in the way that he suggests. Writing is never a matter of a subject that way.)

I will, of course, praise anything my students write on this assignment with any semblance of life to it; I'll praise any set of sentences to which my response as a reader has any trace of: "Yes, that's knowing, that's *his* knowing as he is living it." But what I expect to be working on mainly with this set of papers is why they aren't about anything. I will try, that is, on the basis of this platitudinous claim and that, to trace out the nature of Mr. Corporate Identity, to determine who is speaking in a given paragraph or set of paragraphs, about what, and to whom. I would, for example, with the paper above, ask the students what they made of the fact that for the term "science" one could just as easily read "cookery" or "basket weaving." Could not most of the sentences of the first paragraph be rearranged with no substantial shift in the meaning of it? Is this true also of the sentences of the last two paragraphs? Could paragraphs two, three, four, and five in their entirety be similarly shuffled? How about the phraseology: "vast resources of knowledge," "many people walk around acting like machines," and so on—does any of it sound familiar? Where do such phrases come from? Who uses such language? Who listens to it with interest? And finally, I would ask the students what they imagined the writer of the paper learned from having written it? What then is the paper good for? Why would anyone want to write it at all?

I don't intend to be savage in my manner about this: "What do you think it means to be derivative, anyway; what do you think sheep are, for Christ's sake?" It's the sheepish grin of acknowledgment I'll be after in the way I'll try to go at things: "O.K., if you really aren't the Jolly Green Giant or a Cub Scout, then why do you sound that way; why do you sound like her; why does she sound like you?" Or: "Isn't the real problem here that you're boring because you're bored and bored because you're boring?" I won't say to the students that on the basis of what they've written, part of the reason why they point where they do is that they can't seem to help it, but I would like our class to suggest that what has been pointed to in this set of papers is more an arrangement of clichés than an idea, more an easy abstraction than a life. What they make of why this is so I will leave to them.

4. A Change of Mind

A common way of speaking of a moment of learning something is to say, "I changed my mind." Let it be granted that we do not say this about all acts of learning, but about some we certainly do. Here is a section of a poem which can be read as a description of such a moment.

One summer evening (led by her°) I found
A little boat tied to a willow tree
Within a rocky cove, its usual home.
Straight I unloosed her chain, and stepping in
Pushed from the shore. It was an act of stealth
And troubled pleasure, nor without the voice
Of mountain-echoes did my boat move on;
Leaving behind her still, on either side,
Small circles glittering idly in the moon,
Until they melted all into one track
Of sparkling light. But now, like one who rows,
Proud of his skill, to reach a chosen point
With an unswerving line, I fixed my view
Upon the summit of a craggy ridge,
The horizon's utmost boundary; far above
Was nothing but the stars and the grey sky.
She was an elfin pinnace; lustily
I dipped my oars into the silent lake,
And, as I rose upon the stroke, my boat
Went heaving through the water like a swan;
When, from behind that craggy steep till then
The horizon's bound, a huge peak, black and huge,
As if with voluntary power instinct,
Upreared its head. I struck and struck again,
And growing still in stature the grim shape
Towered up between me and the stars, and still,
For so it seemed, with purpose of its own
And measured motion like a living thing,
Strode after me. With trembling oars I turned,
And through the silent water stole my way
Back to the covert of the willow tree;
There in her mooring-place I left my bark,—
And through the meadows homeward went, in grave

° Nature.

And serious mood; but after I had seen
That spectacle, for many days, my brain
Worked with a dim and undetermined sense
Of unknown modes of being; o'er my thoughts
There hung a darkness, call it solitude
Or blank desertion. No familiar shapes
Remained, no pleasant images of trees,
Of sea or sky, no colours of green fields;
But huge and mighty forms, that do not live
Like living men, moved slowly through the mind
By day, and were a trouble to my dreams.

                    —*William Wordsworth* *

From the speaker's point of view, and right from the start ("It was
an act of stealth/And troubled pleasure"), his taking the boat for a row
on the lake seems to have felt like a kind of stealing. He takes the boat
anyway, but then after rowing for a while apparently changes his mind
about what he is doing and returns it. The following questions are for the
purpose of helping you determine what seems to be involved in Wordsworth's creation of this experience seen as a change of mind.

After taking the boat, how does the speaker seem at first to feel
about what he is doing? How does he describe his surroundings, for example? What seems to be his attitude toward the boat, the act of rowing?

How does the speaker name his surroundings finally? What state of
mind does his new terminology for his surroundings seem to suggest he
is in?

What is it exactly that decides the speaker to return the boat, that
seems to change his mind about what he is doing? There is that "huge
peak," but is it possible for a detail of landscape to bring about a change
of mind?

                    *   *   *

Write an account as if it were a scene in a short story of a moment
in your experience when you learned something and said (or now feel
you could have said), "I changed my mind." Give all the relevant par-
ticulars. Tell where you were, what was going on, what you were doing,
who else was there, what happened, how you changed your mind.

To judge from what you have written, what exactly was involved in
this learning experience? There was a change. You saw things one way
and then you saw things another way. But what exactly was this mind
you changed? From what to what did you change it?

What do you now say that the phrase "to change your mind" means?

* From William Wordsworth, *The Prelude,* Book One, lines 357–400.

Commentary

I'll begin by collecting the papers addressed to Assignment 5 and have the students write a paper addressing Assignment 6 to be turned in at the next class meeting.

*   *   *

The opportunity to write something other than a Theme for this paper ("as if it were a scene in a short story") I expect will call up from most students only another demonstration of their habit of writing by formula, and it is this that I will be confronting them with in class. I think very few students at this point in the course will be able to imagine that there is much of a problem with the issue of this assignment at all. The mechanism of what is involved in a change of mind is about as far as I expect most of them to get ("I used to think/but now I see"), a mechanism they will simply illustrate rather than explore. Hence I don't think we will find more than stick figures, cartoon characters, moving in our students' prose—like the before and after representations of an Anacin ad. I doubt that in the majority of papers we are going to have much trouble substituting "bicycle riding" for "stamp collecting" or whatever. The moment of the change of mind, if it is not buried altogether ("Then I began to see why women's liberation was important"), I expect will be glossed over by one variety or another of the undramatic writer's "Lo," "and then," "suddenly," "all at once," and so on. There is no question, of course, that that moment is languageless, a languageless gap, and in this sense deeply mysterious (see Wordsworth's "When . . . a huge peak"), but I do not imagine that students are going to have any sense whatever of the mystery of this moment, let alone a way of acknowledging it ("what happened?"). It is this sort of unconsciousness of what language can do and what it cannot (and of what that unconsciousness breeds) that I will be talking about in class as a reversion to formula. The habit of Themewriting (and of the way of seeing implied by it), I hope our session will say, is made a lot more easily than the consequences of having made it are understood—or than the habit itself is broken.

But I also want to spend some time in this class making some connections between a change of mind understood as a metaphor ("what exactly was this mind you changed") with both our nominal and our real subjects—that is, with the fact that all acts of learning would seem to involve an alteration in mind of some sort (whether we speak of them that way or not) and with the ways in which an alteration in mind can be seen as a change in language, a shift in terminology or definition, the replacement of one vocabulary (or syntax) by another. In the selection from *The Prelude,* for example, it is not the "huge peak" as just a detail of landscape that changes the speaker's mind about what he is doing. It is what Wordsworth turns that peak into that brings about the change, his personification of the peak ("upreared its head") as a striding, "living thing"—a personification slid into beautifully with "black and huge,/As if with voluntary power instinct" which modifies the peak as both inanimate and animate simultaneously. It is an act of naming that as a consequence renders a number of other names inadequate for the speaker ("No familiar shapes/Remained, no pleasant images"). A change of mind about a landscape becomes a change of mind about an act becomes a change of mind about the nature of things becomes a change of mind about who one is. I do not mean that I expect students to write like Wordsworth. My point is simply that no matter how bad the students' papers addressing this assignment may be, if it is a change in mind that a writer is talking about, it will be possible to demonstrate in class that that change in mind took place just as Wordsworth's did: as the result of a new set of terms, another language for seeing, feeling, thinking about what was earlier looked at differently. With this assignment, or rather with the issues of it, we are suggesting not only the connection of language with learning, but also the connection of language and learning with identity as well. (Is the Wordsworth who took the boat the same Wordsworth who returned it? Can ever again for him a bird's song sound the same?) I do not expect the students to be very clear about these connections or to make very much of them—not yet. That we have raised possibilities to be made sense of is, at this point, enough.

5. Rote Learning

Go back to the remarks of Wayne Booth quoted in Assignment 3. Consider the kind of learning he says he poured into those papers on the Okies and race relations: "Every opinion was derivative; every observation second-hand." This is usually known as rote-learned knowledge or as rote learning.

Consider your attitudes toward rote learning. How much of your past education would you say has consisted of it? (This question asks for a quantitative answer and you can only make an estimate.) How are you accustomed to hearing it talked about? Are you used to hearing it praised by your teachers, by your family, by your fellow students? Or is it something you expect to hear condemned? How do you feel about it yourself?

Commentary

I'll begin by collecting the papers addressed to Assignment 6, which the students by this time should understand will mean we'll be talking over excerpts from them the next period we meet. I'll remind them anyway.

*   *   *

As I've already suggested in my remarks on the assignments and the course in general, I think that the students' attitudes toward rote learning as they will express them in their papers will emerge as almost totally rote-learned—and this with virtually no consciousness of the ironic self-indictment that such a stance implies. For in spite of our talk about the mysteriousness of the learning process, I would be surprised not to find the most predictable sort of disparagement here: how awful "sheer memorization" is, how rote learning is nothing other than a "mechanical" process, a matter only of "simple repetition," the "unthinking absorption of facts," and so on. I hope that asking them about their own education (as enacted in their writing?) and referring them to their sources (family, teachers, fellow students) may give a few students pause, but my experience leads me to believe that the majority here will jump happily back into the wallow and that we will be lucky as readers even to be able to tell one paper from another. (One of the "papers" I will handle in class for this assignment, incidentally, will be made up of fifteen or twenty sentences that I'll put together from as many student Themes so that the final result will *look* like a paper. I'll talk over this portmanteau paper with the class, at first just as though it were a real one. Then I'll tell them what it is. Then I'll ask them to tell me what my having been able to construct it means about what they did with the assignment.)

What I will be coming at on the basis of what the students have to say about the problem of this assignment is what I feel will be their tendency to oversimplified pronouncement. To the assertion that rote learning is No Good because it does not involve "Thinking," for example, I will respond with a request for clarification, possibly with a request for a demonstration. If rote learning does not involve thought, what does it involve? What does thought involve? Or I will want to know why someone should assume that rote learning implies the opposite of understanding. Can there be understanding without rote learning? Can you describe the opposite of rote learning? Or if rote learning is trivial or unimportant, does that then mean that it doesn't matter whether a mathematician knows that 4 follows 3, that 7 comes before 8? What I hope to lead up to is the question of how much of the terminology of their papers and of our discussion of rote learning in class (ostensibly applying to the opposite of rote learning) would the most pejorative of their definitions for rote learning apply to. What will students really understand by their use of a term such as "understanding"? What will they know about their use of a word like "knowledge"? To judge from this paragraph and that, how much "imagination" and "creativity" lie behind this writer's incantatory mouthings of those exact same words?

6. Rote Learning and History

Here is an anecdote about Charles Edward Garman as a student in the Yale Divinity School. (The date is about 1872.)

> Early in the session . . . Professor Fisher asked us to read fifty pages in his book, *The Beginnings of Christianity,* and the next day called on Garman to recite first. Garman began with the first line and went through to the end of the hour *verbatim et literatim.**

This is told in admiration, as evidence of a fine mind, a remarkable intelligence. Plainly, at one time in the educational system the exact use of the memory was highly valued. It is not so long ago, not much more than forty years, that Yale University operated on the systems of "recitations." Although reciting what has been learned in the textbook has not been much used in colleges and schools for some time, it was probably the rule for most of the 19th century and for many centuries before that. Interestingly, when Garman became a professor himself, he did not use the recitation method.

Suppose that in one of your classes someone began to recite page after page of the "outside readings." There would be no question here of cheating. How would such a frank display of the memory be greeted by teacher and students? How would you respond to it?

What do you suppose has happened in the world? Why is the recitation no longer the normal way of conducting a class? Look at this problem historically: What has happened since 1872 or thereabouts?

Commentary

There is no paper to collect this time, but at the beginning of the period I'll tell students to prepare Assignment 7 (much as they did Assignment 2) for a class discussion the next period we meet. I'm going to call the students' attention particularly to the last paragraph of part two of the assignment ("Look back at the papers you have written for this course so far"). I'm going to tell them that when they come to class, I'll expect them to have specific sections of specific papers to quote from and to be ready to talk about—or to have specific reasons why among their papers there are no such sections to talk about.

* From *Letters, Lectures, and Addresses of Charles Edward Garman,* Boston, 1909, p. 13.

As with Assignment 5, Assignment 6 is another opportunity for the students to confront some of their assumptions about the learning process. It is also a chance for them to become conscious of their language while they are using it in such a way as to become aware of the source and nature of those assumptions. I would hope, that is, that by this time I might have one or two students attuned enough to the feel of a cliché to catch themselves in the act of saying that what is rote-learned is quickly forgotten, or that rote learning takes no understanding, or that the complex and advanced state of knowledge of our present modern day world can no longer simply be memorized in order to meet the challenges of tomorrow. This is what I would hope. It is not what I expect. For in spite of our suggestion in the assignment that the exact use of the memory has for centuries been a valued educational principle (and isn't it still?), again I do not think that we will get much more on this set of papers than the silliest sort of certainty about how some kind of learning (what kind?) is plainly better than some other kind of learning, about how one way of exercising the mind is more beneficial or of more moment than some other way of exercising it. And along with this, I'm afraid, will come the worst sorts of historical chauvinism: since the recitation system no longer exists (anywhere?), it therefore was Bad; what we have today (and what is that?) is Good because progress is civilization's most important product; and so on. I will praise any paper in which anyone suggests that he might have more than a single response to a display such as Garman's. I will praise any bewilderment (faced as bewilderment) with the question of what has happened since 1872 or thereabouts. For I do not think that we are asking our students on this assignment to know exactly how they would respond to a prodigious feat of memorization, any more than we are asking them to know what has happened in the world since 1872 (what has?). We are asking them to recognize the cop-out involved in pretending that one *does* know such things, particularly when the pretense is phrased with the very sort of rote-learned stock talk and betrays the same parrot-mindedness that one claims to be beyond.

I don't intend to beat my students up about what I expect they will do with this assignment, but I do want to use the period to make them as uneasy as I can with the smug generalization. Again, my approach will be interrogative. What makes you so sure that Garman *didn't* understand what he recited; and what, just by the way, do you think that a recitation consisted of? Do you really imagine that people were *asked* to memorize fifty pages a night? Even in 1872? Garman did not himself as a teacher use the recitation system, no; but might there have been any reason for this other than his thinking it was a bad system? What must a teacher who used the recitation system have been able to take for granted that his students could do for themselves, for example? What might Garman as a teacher have believed it was no longer possible to take for granted that students could do for themselves? Memorization is not necessarily a measure of intelligence. Agreed. Similarly, we all know that grades are not necessarily a measure of intelligence either. Why then do the engineers, say, with the highest grades get the best jobs when they leave college? Do you know something that the modern present day world of industry does not know? These modern present day teachers you speak of who work on making their students "think" or "apply knowledge": how exactly do they go about doing this? Is there any way in which being "made to think" is being made to rote-learn? You detest rote learning. As you look at your experience in this course, how would you say you have responded so far to the demand that you produce something other than what you have rote-learned? With a sense of excitement? Joy? There is no involvement in rote learning, you say, no individuality involved in it; it is no more than parrot talk, easily forgotten. Now, read back over the paper you wrote addressing Assignment 6 with those generalizations in mind. Is there any way in which your paper may be called an example of what you have defined as rote learning? Garman memorized a section of one of his teacher's books (and why, do you suppose?). Evidently he was quite conscious of what he was doing. To judge from the paper you wrote addressing Assignment 6, what have you memorized? How conscious were you in memorizing what you did? In reproducing it? Might Garman have learned anything worth knowing from his rote learning? How about what you have learned from yours?

7. The Telephone Dial (Part I)

We turn now to an example of your own rote learning. Do you remember how old you were when you first learned to use the telephone? And you have been using it ever since, for fifteen years, more or less, how many times a month, a week, a day?

The circular dialing mechanism of the telephone is an apparatus with which you have had a great deal of experience. You can close your eyes and visualize it, can you not? Half asleep you could call Seattle. Or Bangkok. Perhaps you are so familiar with the telephone that you could dial a number in the dark if you had to. Why, a mere child . . .

Take ten minutes or so right now in order to sketch from memory the standardized circular dialing mechanism that you use so often and know so well. Include all the numbers and letters as you remember them. The right-angled coordinates below are for the purpose of enabling you to make your circles as true as possible. Scale your model in any way that you wish, but try to keep the various parts of your model as proportionate to one another as you can. When you've gone as far with your sketch as you think you can go, turn to Part II of this assignment.

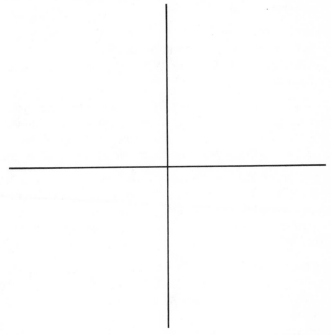

7. The Telephone Dial (Part II)

Check the sketch you made of the dialing mechanism of the telephone against the real thing. Did you make any mistakes? Of what sort? (The usual number of errors, by the way, is about two dozen.) Did you know that there was no dialing hole at twelve o'clock? Did you remember that the letters Q and Z are not used in the system? How about the relationship of the numbers to the letters, did you get that right? Does your sketch indicate that the lettering order reverses itself at M? The little white (or black) dot at the center of the dialing holes: Was that in your drawing? Did you know that that dot cost the telephone company upward of a quarter of a million dollars in research money to place where it is, and that it is said to save the company millions of dollars a year in preventing misplaced telephone calls? Could your sketch of the telephone dial serve as the model for a telephone? Could you call Seattle on such a telephone?

If you made mistakes in your sketch, how do you account for the fact that you made the mistakes you did? Can you see any pattern in them? Do you think that after checking your sketch against the dial that you could make a more accurate model than you first did. Why? Are there some mistakes you are convinced you wouldn't, won't, make a second time? Why?

There are certain details of the telephone dial that you got right in your sketch, that almost anybody would. Which ones? How do you account for the fact that you got them right, for your certainty that almost anyone would?

Perhaps there are certain details you got right that you are not convinced everybody would. If so, if you knew for certain what letters weren't used in the dialing system, for example, how did you know it? What makes you uncertain whether others would know what you know?

You will notice that this assignment is worded in such a way as to allow for the possibility of someone's having made an accurate sketch of the telephone dial. Speculate for a moment on who such a person might be? Are such terms as Genius, Photographic Memory, Mental Picture, and the like of much help to you with such a question?

You have rote-learned how to use the telephone dialing mechanism. (Is it something you really know?) You know what the telephone dial looks like. But what is it that you rote-learned? What is it that you show in your sketch you knew, exactly?

Look back at the papers you have written for this course so far. To judge from what you have written, have you rote-learned anything else in the way that you rote-learned the telephone dial? What does your way of addressing this question enable you to conclude about your relationship to your learning?

Commentary

At the opening of class, I'll tell the students to prepare Assignment 8 for discussion at our next meeting.

*   *   *

I would like Assignment 7 to dramatize from a different point of view an idea I will only have touched on with the Wordsworth selection in Assignment 4: namely, that our experience is not what we experience, everything we experience, in just those terms; what we learn or know of the world is what we make the world into. We experience, in other words, what we *tell* ourselves that we have experienced, what we have in some way verbalized to ourselves in some form of language. From this point of view, what I know or remember is not objects or events or people, but the languages with which I have made sense of objects, events, and people, the symbol systems with which I have given them shape and meaning. The world does not happen to me, at least in the way that the term "world" is ordinarily understood, as a synonym for Reality or Isness. I happen to the world. This is why language, my language, is important.

My children, for example, are so many years old, were born in such and such years. I know their ages immediately, but invariably, for income tax forms and the like, I have to stop to figure out that they were born in 1961 and 1963.* I do not experience them in that way. Similarly, not very many people (try this with your students) can with their eyes closed answer the question of where the ears on a human head are attached: above a horizontal line bisecting the face, below it, or just about on the line. But if you've studied art, drawing, you will know immediately (and know that you know) that the answer is about on the line. By the same token, the chances are that those students who on this assignment know that the letters Q and Z are not used in the dialing mechanism of the telephone will not only know that they know it, but how ("I heard it asked on a quiz program once"; "I once had to find numerical equivalents for each letter and I noticed then"). The point is that in all these instances what is remembered is not what one has "seen" (how many ears have all of us looked at?); what is remembered is one's experience

* My wife, after typing this, reminded me that our daughters were born in 1962 and 1964. See what I mean?

with a language for what he has seen. (Cellini in his *Autobiography* recalls his father's once boxing his ears, and afterwards giving him some money, so that he would not forget the experience of watching a salamander's being "born" from the coals of the family fireplace.)

The implications of all this, when I put them in terms of the relationship of language to the responsibility I am forced to acknowledge I must assume for the shape of my life, are to me staggering. I *can*, of course, figure out the years in which my children were born, just as I can check a sketch of the telephone dial against the telephone dial. But where for me now are all those rich experiences I must have had in third or fourth grade? Where are all those lesser known Shakespeare plays that I've read but was never "made" to write papers on and never talked over with anyone? Why is it that when I go tiptoeing back through a diary I kept in high school and come upon the entry: "With Marilyn tonight: the greatest yet"—I can no more remember that night than I can what was great about it? I don't care about how I know the telephone dial, but I do care, and I hope that some of my students may, that to go through life Themewriting my experience into bloodless abstractions—we had a swell time; she was really cool; it was a great trip—is to end up finally with a great deal of that life having trickled through my fingers.

When the students come to class they will already, presumably, have sketched the dialing mechanism of the telephone from memory once. They will also have looked at their sketches in the light of the questions on Part Two of the assignment. I'm going to begin class by asking the students to close their books and to take ten or fifteen minutes to sketch the mechanism again. I then plan to have the class use these on-the-spot sketches to address the questions on Part Two of the assignment about mistakes one wouldn't make a second time.

Unless I'm very badly mistaken, what I think I'll find is that most of the students in their second sketches will have the little white or black dot, that not quite as many will remember that Q and Z aren't used in the system, but that very few will be able to reproduce exactly the way in which the lettering order reverses itself at M (which I myself couldn't do right now; I'm going to have to check it carefully before I go to class). The reason for this is that we have boxed the students' ears with the little white or black dot (look at how much we've told them about it), whereas we've said very little about the reversal of the lettering at M.

What the students will be remembering, then, I'll be arguing, is not having "seen" the dot or their Mental Picture of it, whatever that is (they "saw" the letters reversing too); they will be remembering the language we've given them about the dot. I want then to move to the question of what everyone got right in the sketch even the first time (the roundness of the dialing holes, the grouping of letters into threes, the appearance of the word "operator," etc.). The point I will be trying to make here (and which I hope the last two paragraphs on Part Two of the assignment will give us a specific way of talking about) is that what we rote-learn about the telephone dial is very much like what I think the students will have shown they rote-learned about history in what they said in their papers on Assignment 6 (and in other papers too, of course— in any paper where someone's experience is reduced to clichés; I'll be interested to see what sections of which papers they select to talk about). They did not on Assignment 6 simply repeat what was said to them (it is hard, for example, to imagine any teacher's having ever said to a class that no one knew anything about education before the Twentieth Century in just those terms). What the students reproduced on Assignment 6 was what they had turned a teacher's remarks, or the prose of a textbook, into—in the same way that what they recorded in their first sketches of the telephone dial is not what the telephone dial looks like, but the lowest common denominator of its appearance. In both their remarks on history and their sketches of the telephone dial, then, the students will have written clichés. So far as the telephone dial is concerned, who cares; but I hope to leave with them the question of who might care when it comes to their relationship to the rest of their experience.

8. Rote Learning and Writing

To return to the notion that there are some things you really know, what about writing? Can a knowledge of writing be part of a writer? Can a knowledge of writing be rote-learned? What does it mean to say that it can or cannot?

Let's look at some examples of writing as a way of trying to address these questions. Again, our approach will be historical. We will confine ourselves to the writing of students, all of whom wrote what they did in circumstances much like those in which you find yourself as a student in this course. They were writing required papers for a course in composition.

Here, for instance, is a section of a student's paper submitted in a writing course at Harvard in 1893:

The Paradise of Books

Books, I often think, are the best thing life has to offer us. No where else do we get pleasure that is so great and so lasting, that can charm us still, whatever our condition of mind and body. There we meet friends and lovers such as reality cannot acquaint us with, and adventures which furnish excitement without toil, and arouse sympathy without suffering. All the higher emotions, so incongruous with matter-of-fact existence, may be serenely enjoyed in the realm of poetry, and all the speculative flights which transcend cold common-sense may soar undisturbed in the aether of philosophy. As long as a man has eyes to read and brain to understand, he may feel sure of one unfailing resource which can amply compensate the strokes of fortune.

Here is a section of a paper written by a student in the early 1960s:

What is the alternative to the conflict between nation and nation, Black and White, Gentile and Jew, Parent and Child? It is to put the flower in the gun, to grow a little more sensitive to the needs of others, a little less selfish in the attempt to communicate. It is to recognize that materialism breeds only materialism, and hatred hatred. It is to see as Jesus and Mohammed saw that the needs of mankind can be met . . .

Later in the same decade a student wrote:

Too much violence, eh? What we don't have is enough. Look at King. Look at the Kennedys. Where are they now? Look at what happened to the "Niggers" in Detroit. Look at where wanting the vote got the people of Mississippi. We'll "overcome" when we start to understand that violence is the only thing the People of the United States will listen to. It's the poor and the hungry, those who are jammed into ghettoes by acts of corruption and inequalities of . . .

And not so long ago, a student wrote this:

I believe that the past is tremendously important to the success or failure of everyone later on in his life. My past has taught me many valuable lessons which I will not easily forget. The most important lesson I have learned to date would be with regards to patience. As a boxer will tell you, you have to learn to roll with every punch your opponent throws at you. It is the same in day to day life situations. You should be aware of all around you and keep a relatively rational mind so you can make the right decisions.

How would you characterize the voice you hear speaking in each of the passages above? How do you respond to those voices in each instance? What would you say that the ideal audience for the voice in each case would be? Do you find yourself a member of any of these audiences ever?

The examples given you span almost a century. There are obvious differences between them. But it is also possible to draw some connecting lines here, to see those pieces of writing in similar terms. What terms do you use to connect them? What lines do you draw?

How do you think the writers of each of the passages learned to write as they did? Who do you think taught them, and how was this teaching done? And how about the learning, how was that done?

Commentary

At the beginning of class, I'll tell the students to prepare Assignment 9 for a discussion at our next meeting. I'll also tell them to write a paper addressing Assignment 10 to be turned in at that same meeting.

*　　*　　*

What I did in order to put this exercise together was to dredge from my files some good working definitions of emptiness as I've collected them through the years. My intent is to create a vantage point from which to see Themewriting as a generic term and as other than a local phenomenon. Writing by formula, journalism (the writing of a sentence which writes the next ten sentences for you), is writing by formula—whether one chooses to sound like a New Orleans taxicab driver or a blue chip stock. The parameters, as the social scientists say, are really negligible. It doesn't matter whether the prose is bell-bottomed or cut like a Brooks Brothers suit. The subject could be the legalization of grass or abortion, the fraternity system or gay liberation. What does matter is that in each case here the prose isn't prose, the subjects aren't subjects, the voices aren't voices. What matters is that in each instance the writing isn't writing and the chances are that the writers don't know it. I've tried, in other words, to provide us with a range of badness that we can kick around with the students in the classroom as a way of dramatizing to one another that we're all done with such greasy kid stuff. (That we won't be doesn't touch what I see as the educational value of the gesture.)

Since it is possible to move from any one of these four pieces of junk to any of the others, I'll handle this exercise in class by asking the students which one they'd like to start with (I want to see what they've been able to rote-learn about how to evaluate an order of words on a page). The Harvard student's paper I think they'll probably steer around, but I'd like to take them to it through what I hope they'll notice about the other three selections: that the voice of each is completely imitable (I'll have them make up some sentences in class to add to each selection, sentences that they'd call indistinguishable in tone and manner from the rest of the paragraph, in order to demonstrate this); that each one of them is made up of catch phrases rather than words; that the ordering principle of each selection is not much more than the ordering principle of a shopping list (what sentence of the fourth selection couldn't you begin the paragraph with? what details of the other two couldn't you switch around or find equivalents for?), and that as a consequence any one of the selections could be either cut in half or swelled to ten times its length through the application of a simple formula ("All you'd have to do is put in some more opposites" "All you'd have to do is get some more examples of injustice"), and so on—this listing is by no means exhaustive. I hope to use this discussion to come at the trick of the Harvard student's paper by asking the students where they think they'd find someone who really believed what that writer claims to believe in that paper. Is the opposition, for example, between "the higher emotions" and "matter-of-fact existence" indeed that simple for anyone? Was it that simple in 1893? Outside of an institution, was there anyone ever who imagined that a book could "amply compensate" for, say, the death of a parent or a friend? Is the Harvard student's paper any more believable as the utterance of a human voice than the stock protests against inequality in the third selection, the simple-minded formula for peace and prosperity in the second? It's with questions such as these that I'll then move to asking the students to speculate on why they imagine that such papers were written to begin with. Who is such writing for? Where would it be taken seriously? (All these questions, I think, involve the issues of teaching and learning that we invite the students to consider with the final paragraph of the assignment). In the midst of what I imagine will be the happy mob rush to decry the School System and to burn Mizgrundy ("They *make* you write like that in high school") I want to recall very quietly our discussion on the dialing mechanism of the telephone by raising the question of whether students are *made* to write by formula or whether what was offered the students in high school was *made into* a demand that they write by formula. For I do not believe that anyone gets sold down the river that way without in some sense wanting to make the trip.

9. Children's Writing

It has been said that the difference between a child's and an adult's writing is not that one is good and the other bad, for they both may be bad. But a child's writing sometimes shows "a clarity of vision, [a] force of expression, [and] . . . an innocence of imagination that adults might envy." It is also declared that most "children find it hard to go on writing interestingly. . . . Of a sudden, the child is a child no longer" (Boris Ford *).

Boris Ford, you will note, is not a sentimentalist. Children's writing can be bad:

Christmas Eve

It was Christmas Eve.
When you looked out the window
   you could see the lights.
When you looked all around it was
   a beautiful sight.
You could hear bells ringing,
   You could hear people singing.
The snow was so white
 . Everything was so bright,
   It was a beautiful sight!

—Dana, age 10

But look at this writing done by children. Both Kathy and Michael are average students—so far as such a term ever meant anything.

If I Were the Snow

If I were the snow
I would snow every
single Christmas.
I would snow on my
brother and make his
toes so red he
would hit me.
I would snow all over the
universe, on Mars,

---

* Boris Ford, *Young Writers, Young Readers,* London, 1960, p. 97. Reprinted by permission of Humanities Press, Inc., New York.

the earth. I would
snow so hard on
the moon, I
would show the man
on there who's boss.
I would not be just white
I'd be red, blue, and
green. I'd be yellow
dots, orange dots
black ones too.

—*Kathy, age 10* †

Sums

One and Two were playing about in a sum-book. Suddenly One said, 'I'm older than you because I am fifty, you are only ten!'

Of course Two was very angry. 'I've had enough of you!'

'But that was only in the game,' protested One.

'Game or no game, I've had enough of you. You can go out of here at once!'

'Boo-Hoo! Don't want to go out of here; want to stay here; boo-hoo!'

'Well, you're going out of here!' And Two pushed One out and slammed the door behind him, and locked it firmly!

That evening Twenty came home from work, tired and angry. 'Where is One?' he shouted. (One always pulled up Twenty's chair.)

'Well, father . . .' began Two, when Twenty interrupted: 'No "wells," where is he?'

'Well, father,' began Two again. 'Well, father, we had a quarrel, and I pushed One out!'

'What? Well bring him in!'

So Two went out, and half an hour later came back with One. 'Here he is father,' said Two.

'Good,' thundered father.

Some days later, One and Two were playing. 'I'm older than you,' said One.

'O.K., have it your own way!' said Two.

—*Michael, age 9* ‡

† From *Wishes, Lies and Dreams*, by Kenneth Koch and the Students of P.S. 61 in New York City. Copyright © 1970 by Kenneth Koch. Reprinted by permission of Random House, Inc.

‡ In Boris Ford, *Young Writers, Young Readers, op. cit.,* p. 8.

What do you make of these two pieces? Though you are not accustomed, perhaps, to seeing your study of calculus or physics, say, in relation to your home life or your social situation; though you may not ordinarily think of snow in terms of Mars or colored polka dots—these pieces aren't exactly silly, are they? Do you see anything in them, anything specific, that you might want to call "a clarity of vision" or a "force of expression" or an "innocence of imagination?" Is there anything here you "envy"?

Ford uses the term "child" to make a distinction between ways of seeing and experiencing the world. There is the "child" and then there is "the child [who] is a child no longer." On the basis of your experience with these three pieces of children's writing, explain your understanding of this distinction.

Commentary

I'll begin class by collecting the students' papers addressed to Assignment 10, which we'll take up at our next meeting.

*   *   *

Though it may not happen right away (and with some students it may never happen at all), with this assignment there is a chance of putting a student into a position to say to himself what we could never say to him and be believed in any way that would make much difference: "good writing, writing that is interesting, arresting, alive, is not a matter of some special gift or talent conveyed at birth. It's a matter of seeing, and since seeing is a matter of teaching and learning, how one sees is a matter of choice as well. If children, ordinary children, can write as these children do, then perhaps the demand being made on me by this course is neither impossible nor meaningless. Perhaps I am being asked no more as a writer than that I make some effort to see what I can see (and for myself, not for someone else), some effort to distinguish between what I see and what I have been told (and told myself) that I ought to see. The value of this may be to put me into closer touch with myself through the touch I'm able to make with the world around me." Sentences like that for students, realizations of that sort, are a long way off. But if anything like such a realization is ever to come to any of them, someone somewhere along the line has to begin behaving as though he believed such a thing were possible.

Through this assignment and through our behavior with it in class I think we have a chance to do this, for what I see both Kathy and Michael enacting in their writing, and what I'd like to dramatize to the students with it, is the opposite of the dissociated sensibility. The quality of their writing for me creates the image of someone able to see Spinoza, the sound of the typewriter, and the smell of cooking as having something to do with one another. After our class on Assignment 8, I don't think that the students should have much trouble seeing the selection by Dana as a Theme (though I think that just to make sure I'll ask them how much of that poem they'd have to change to make it seem to apply to the Fourth of July), but I think that the chief difficulty we're going to have in handling the last two selections is in getting the students to find, as Wittgenstein would put it, some substance for Ford's substantives, getting them to develop some terminology for what it is that they hear. "Simple and direct," "original," "vividness of imagination"—it's this sort of rhetoric that I imagine we'll be pushing the students to find correlatives for.

I expect we'll also have to deal with the silliness of supposing that Michael and Kathy are writing Moral Messages (and what assumptions about childhood are behind such a statement?)—which I plan to handle by asking about the response Kathy imagines for her brother (I'll play devil's advocate here and call her sadistic), and by asking the students what they make of the fact that you can't tell whether *Sums* is written from the point of view of One or of Two. But I'm counting on most of the students being delighted with the last two selections, and it's in trying to find a language for that delight that I expect we'll be spending most of the period. And I mean "we." For I have no ready-made language for what I respond to in those pieces any more than I have a ready-made way for talking about any piece of art I admire. In fact, my point in class is going to be precisely that this *is* my difficulty as a reader of them. Once I see the dust-jacket rhetoric ("vividness") as inadequate to approach the writing here as writing, the terminology and techniques I turn to (such as seeing whether "No 'wells,' where is he?" can be read aloud with more than one kind of inflection) are like those that I would use to talk about art I took seriously as art. In other words, the in-adequacy I feel of my language to do justice to my sense of the vitality, honesty, unashamed wonderment (more dust-jacket rhetoric) of those pieces is a measure of their quality, of what has been achieved in them. To describe a voice of one's own I need my own voice, and for that there is no formula. No, I plan to conclude class by observing that I do not always see my experiences as a teacher in relation to my experiences as a father or *vice versa,* but writing like Kathy's and Michael's not only makes me aware that it is possible, it makes me aware of who I might be in realizing the possibility. "Envy" seems a good word, envy (in my case at any rate) that is born of longing.

10. The Theme: What Is It?

You know what a sonnet is. Perhaps you can define the terms *short story, novel, play, epic*. Maybe you even know how to describe the heroic couplet as used by Alexander Pope or blank verse by Shakespeare. In other words, you do know something about Literary Forms.

Consider the Literary Form known as *The English Paper* or *Theme*. No one leaves high school without knowing about Themewriting or without knowing how to write a Theme. Indeed, the technique can sometimes be learned a great deal earlier, as early as the age of ten.

Themewriting is a language, a way of experiencing the world. It is nonwriting rather than writing.

Invented originally by English teachers for use in English classrooms only, it is as closed a language as the Dewey Decimal System, as calculatedly dissociated from the concerns of its user and the world he lives in as it has been possible to make it. But the selling points of it as a commodity are irresistible. For since the skill of Themewriting is based upon the use of language conceived of entirely in terms of communication, the only standard that need be applied to it is whether it succeeds in creating in the reader—that is, in another Themewriter—the desired response. The writer's character, personality, moral nature, convictions . . . it is taken for granted are in no way engaged in forming sentences out of words and paragraphs out of sentences. Language is a tool, it is said. Or just a tool. If the reader buys the product or the idea, believes something, feels certain emotions, votes a particular ticket, etc., then the writing is good. Then the English is good.

The selling points of this commodity are not only irresistible, they are undeniable; and so is the utility of what is being sold. Writing seen as a trick that can be played, a device that can be put into operation, is also a technique that can be taught and learned— just as one can be taught or can learn to run an adding machine, or pour concrete. And once equipped with this skill a writer can write a Theme about anything, and at a moment's notice. It is a valuable technique to know, therefore, because like the American dollar it is negotiable anywhere—and its buying power is unlimited. A student can use the technique of Themewriting not only to write papers but to plan a career or a marriage, to organize a life even. And if the standards of this imitation writing are those to which the dignity of full commitment is unthinkable; if the orders won by it are more sterile than the chaos from which they are won; if the price paid to teach this kind of writing, and to learn it, may be more than the chance to be Lively or Interesting; there are few to say so. For to make Themewriting or non-writing stand for writing . . . is to make impossible also the conception of, let alone the demand for, writing as writing inside its circle.

—William E. Coles, Jr.*

With Themewriting it is possible not only "to organize a life" for one's self, it is possible also to organize—that does seem the right word —a life for others. Consider the following remarks by George Orwell (from an essay originally published in 1946):

In our time it is broadly true that political writing is bad writing. Where it is not true, it will generally be found that the writer is some kind of rebel, expressing his private opinions and not a "party line." Orthodoxy, of whatever color, seems to demand a lifeless, imitative style. The political dialects to be found in pamphlets, leading articles, manifestos, White Papers and the speeches of under-secretaries do, of course, vary from party to party, but they are all alike in that one almost never finds in them a fresh, vivid, homemade turn of speech. When one watches some tired hack on the platform mechanically repeating the familiar phrases—*bestial atrocities, iron heel, bloodstained tyranny, free peoples of the world, stand shoulder to shoulder*—one often has a curious feeling that one is not watching a live human being but some kind of dummy: a feeling which suddenly becomes stronger at moments when the light catches the speaker's spectacles and turns them into blank discs which seem to have no eyes behind them. And this is not altogether fanciful. A speaker who uses that kind of phraseology has gone some distance towards turning himself into a machine. The appropriate noises are coming out of his larynx, but his brain is not involved as it would be if he were choosing his words for himself. If the speech he is making is one that he is accustomed to make over and over again, he may be almost unconscious of what he is saying, as one is when one utters the responses in church. And this reduced state of consciousness, if not indispensable, is at any rate favorable to political conformity.

In our time, political speech and writing are largely the defence of the indefensible. Things like the continuance of British rule in India, the Russian purges and deportations, the dropping of the atom bombs on Japan, can indeed be defended, but only by arguments

---

* William E. Coles, Jr., "Freshman Composition: The Circle of Unbelief," *College English,* November, 1969, pp. 136–137. Reprinted with permission of the National Council of Teachers of English.

which are too brutal for most people to face, and which do not square with the professed aims of political parties. Thus political language has to consist largely of euphemism, question-begging and sheer cloudy vagueness. Defenceless villagers are bombarded from the air, the inhabitants driven out into the countryside, the cattle machine-gunned, the huts set on fire with incendiary bullets: this is called *pacification*. Millions of peasants are robbed of their farms and sent trudging along the roads with no more than they can carry: this is called *transfer of population* or *rectification of frontiers*. People are imprisoned for years without trial, or shot in the back of the neck or sent to die of scurvy in Arctic lumber camps: this is called *elimination of unreliable elements*. Such phraseology is needed if one wants to name things without calling up mental pictures of them. . . .

The great enemy of clear language is insincerity. When there is a gap between one's real and one's declared aims, one turns as it were instinctively to long words and exhausted idioms, like a cuttlefish squirting out ink. In our age there is no such thing as "keeping out of politics." All issues are political issues, and politics itself is a mass of lies, evasions, folly, hatred and schizophrenia. When the general atmosphere is bad, language must suffer. I should expect to find—this is a guess which I have not sufficient knowledge to verify—that the German, Russian and Italian languages have all deteriorated in the last ten or fifteen years, as a result of dictatorship.

—*George Orwell* †

*   *   *

In the technique of Themewriting you need no further training. We are entirely satisfied that you can write a Theme on any given subject. This paper will give you an opportunity to demonstrate your skill with the technique of Themewriting, to share some of your trade secrets. It will give you also an opportunity to come to terms with what it means to have such trade secrets to share.

First of all, play the game for a paragraph. Choose what might seem to be three or four disparate words or terms, terms, that is, with no obvious relationship between them, and list them at the head of your paper. Then make a relationship between the terms in the form of a Lead Sentence that will enable you to write a Theme. Come up with a paragraph that will enable a reader to say: "Yes, it looks like English. It looks like a Theme or the start of one written for an English course."

† Excerpted from "Politics and the English Language" in *Shooting an Elephant and Other Essays* by George Orwell, copyright 1945, 1946, 1949, 1950 by Sonia Brownell Orwell. Reprinted by permission of Harcourt Brace Jovanovich, Inc.

Now, consider how you performed this trick, for trick it is. How did you begin? How did you know how to proceed? What state of mind do you assume to write a Theme? What criticisms do you attempt to forestall? What standards do you try to preserve? For whom are you writing? What good is it?

When you have made up your mind about these matters, express your understanding of what you have done in the form of a diagram or drawing. Or, perhaps, you could develop a mathematical or chemical equation. You may use explanatory words or sentences, but express yourself primarily in a language other than English. Use color if you wish.

Finally, write a paragraph in which you attempt to establish your relationship, not to your example of Themewriting, but to your own writing. What is the nature of this relationship as you see it now? Do you wish that it were other than it is? Why? This is a paragraph in which you can look back over what you have been doing so far this term and draw some conclusions.

Commentary

I'll begin class by asking the students to prepare Assignment 11 for our next class meeting. I'll call their attention particularly to the final paragraph, the NB of the assignment, because, though I won't tell the students this, I'm planning to give them a five minute quiz on the life of Malcolm X when we take up Assignment 11 in class. I'll want to see simply who has looked up Malcolm X and who hasn't. Anyone who hasn't I'm going to have do a one page paper on the significance of his life— complete with listed source materials. I don't imagine that this procedure will create a sense of intellectual responsibility in my students, but it can be a way of arguing that this is a course to be taken seriously.

*   *   *

I've devised Assignment 10 to serve as a kind of summation of the first couple of weeks of the course. In it I try to provide the students with an opportunity to see Themewriting as a matter of language and language using in a larger context than most of them seem able to supply for it —at least in terms of their own writing, their own language using. This is the reason for the two quotations, both of which (although in different ways) make an attempt to draw some lines between the use of language and the nature of experience, or more specifically between the debasement of language and the debasement of the sensibility. I've deliberately not asked any questions about either of the passages because it's the way the passages suggest that the connection of language with experience is possible (and not the nature of the connection) that I hope one or two students may wish to take into account and develop their own terms for in that final paragraph we're asking them to write.

The earlier part of the assignment will involve the students in another way of seeing Themewriting as more than a bad habit. By having them construct a diagram which will describe the writing of a Theme as a trick, we are really asking them to move from the English language to another language in order to express themselves. That will be obvious. What I do not think will be so obvious to the students is that in their use of this language other than English, they will be as tempted by the techniques of the Themewriter as they are when they use English—without, of course, realizing that it is clichés they are using, superficies they are dealing in. What I expect of most of their diagrams, in other words, is Themes about Themewriting. Like the Theme, the students' drawings will have a tendency to show a lot of ingenuity without much real thought, a lot of cleverness without much intelligence. At its worst this will take the form of a dust-off (three squares labeled "Introduction," "Body," and "Conclusion"—which doesn't express an understanding of doing at all); at its best, there will be glorious swoops of color and lots of decorative filigree (like the Themewriter's "adding" of "vivid details" to his paper, none of which have any organic connection with the development of a subject). This unconscious Themewriting is the price of having trade secrets of the Themewriter's sort to share. I plan to be respectful of any effort that shows wit or care, but I will also want to talk about how a choice of color or the shapes made by lines can express individuality— or fail to. (I plan here to capitalize on our discussion of Assignment 8, which I hope will have made clear that different kinds of bad writing, writing that at first may not seem discussable with the same terms, may nevertheless be said to have certain common denominators.) "Why does the writer use the color blue here," I imagine myself asking of a drawing, "and not green or red?" Or "All these pieces of garbage drawn here at the bottom of the page: is there anything familiar about representing junk with a rusty tin can?" I hope that this part of the period may at least give pause to the fellow who tells us: "Yeah, my *writing* is filled with clichés, but man like you oughta hear me on Saturday nights when I'm like really me."

In the students' final paragraphs we may get more Themes about how awful Themewriting is, but at this point I really do hope for at least one example of someone's seeing the activity of writing as at least touching on something else in his life. If I don't get anything that I think I can praise in this way, I'll spend the latter part of the period with Orwell.

11. Malcolm X

Here is a description of a learning experience taken from *The Autobiography of Malcolm X.**

The experience spoken of took place toward the beginning of Malcolm X's serving a ten year prison term. He had had only an eighth grade education. In his attempts to write letters about "how the white man's society was responsible for the black man's condition in this wilderness of North America" (he wrote to the Mayor of Boston, the Governor of Massachusetts, and the President of the United States among others), he found himself, as he says, "increasingly frustrated at not being able to express what [he] wanted to convey. . . . In the street," he writes, "I had been the most articulate hustler out there—I had commanded attention when I said something. But now, trying to write simple English, I not only wasn't articulate, I wasn't even functional. How would I sound writing in slang, the way I would *say* it, something such as, 'Look, daddy, let me pull your coat about a cat. . . .' " Also, Malcolm X speaks of his "envy" of a fellow prisoner whose "stock of knowledge" enabled him to "take charge of any conversation he was in." In an attempt "to emulate" this prisoner (these are his words "envy" and "emulate"), Malcolm X tried to read what he could, but in skipping the words he didn't understand, he went through, as he puts it, "only book reading motions" and ended up with "little idea" of the meaning of what he had read. In order "to study, to learn some words" (and also "to improve penmanship"), he requested a dictionary along with some tablets and pencils from the prison school. The following is his account of what happened once these materials had been given to him.

I spent two days just riffling uncertainly through the dictionary's pages. I'd never realized so many words existed! I didn't know *which* words I needed to learn. Finally, just to start some kind of action, I began copying.

In my slow, painstaking, ragged handwriting, I copied into my tablet everything printed on that first page, down to the punctuation marks.

I believe it took me a day. Then, aloud, I read back, to myself, everything I'd written on the tablet. Over and over, aloud, to myself, I read my own handwriting.

* From *The Autobiography of Malcolm X* by Malcolm X with the assistance of Alex Haley. Copyright © 1964 by Alex Haley and Malcolm X; copyright © 1965 by Alex Haley and Betty Shabazz. Reprinted by permission of Grove Press, Inc.

I woke up the next morning, thinking about those words—immensely proud to realize that not only had I written so much at one time, but I'd written words I never knew were in the world. Moreover, with a little effort, I also could remember what many of these words meant. I reviewed the words whose meanings I didn't remember. Funny thing, from the dictionary first page right now, that "aardvark" springs to my mind. The dictionary had a picture of it, a long-tailed, long-eared, burrowing African mammal, which lives off termites caught by sticking out its tongue as an anteater does for ants.

I was so fascinated that I went on—I copied the dictionary's next page. And the same experience came when I studied that. With every succeeding page, I also learned of people and places and events from history. Actually the dictionary is like a miniature encyclopedia. Finally the dictionary's A section had filled a whole tablet—and I went on into the B's. That was the way I started copying what eventually became the entire dictionary. It went a lot faster after so much practice helped me to pick up handwriting speed. Between what I wrote in my tablet, and writing letters, during the rest of my time in prison I would guess I wrote a million words.

Throughout his *Autobiography,* Malcolm X speaks of this experience in tones of unmistakable gratitude. He read books too, of course, and talked with many of his fellow prisoners. He debated and took advantage of classes provided by the prison administration. But the act of copying out the dictionary *verbatim* he specifies as a seminal experience in his education.

*   *   *

Do you believe that Malcolm X did what he says he did? In prison one is likely to have time on his hands to be sure, but the *whole* dictionary? Almost a *million* words? Why do you believe him or disbelieve him?

Suppose Malcolm X actually did exactly what he says he did. To judge only from what you read of his words in this exercise, what would you say his motivation for copying the dictionary was? Would you call his motives admirable? Complex? You will be speculating here, of course, but not just airily supposing; you will be looking, that is, at how you move from words to meaning in Malcolm X's sentences.

It is clear that Malcolm X did not want to write as he talked: "How would I sound writing in slang?" How would he have sounded, and why do you suppose he wasn't satisfied to sound as he thought he would have? Isn't naturalness a virtue?

What do you think Malcolm X did want to sound like? A Theme-writer? The New York Public Library? Any other possibilities?

In addition to copying out the dictionary, Malcolm X suggests that he also read aloud what he had written "over and over." And he sees a connection between these activities and his becoming articulate, a writer and a speaker. (Perhaps with no more than an eighth grade education he was ignorant of what is said to have happened in the world since 1872 or thereabouts?) Do you think that such activities did help him to become a writer? A speaker? What makes you say so, one way or the other?

But suppose someone who knew for sure told you that Malcolm X never became The Writer He Wanted To Be. (Who does?) Suppose you accepted the observation. What then would you say was the effect of the actions involved in his copying out the dictionary? What exactly did Malcolm X rote-learn, anyway? Words? Definitions? The Dictionary? Anything else?

Now, what about you and your education in the light of this description of a learning experience? Can you imagine yourself doing such a thing as copying out the dictionary under any circumstances? Have you ever done anything like that? Have you ever known anyone or of anyone other than Malcolm X who did? With what results? Can you imagine any benefit to your doing such a thing? Any detriment? When it comes to an understanding of such terms as "dictionary," "copying," "read back aloud," and "words," what similarities are there between you and Malcolm X? What are the differences?

*   *   *

N.B. It will be assumed that when you come to class to discuss this assignment you will know who Malcolm X was and know also something about his life, his career, and what he stood for. Be ready to furnish specific information on your references. Hearsay, word-of-mouth information, will not be acceptable. For what reason do you suppose?

Commentary

I'll begin class by telling the students to prepare Assignment 12 for a discussion next period, and then I'll give them a five minute quiz about Malcolm X: "Name any revolutionary movement Malcolm X was associated with." "How did Malcolm X die?" "What major change did Malcolm X make in his philosophy toward the end of his life?" "What printed sources did you use for your information?" And I will also ask the students: "Define the word 'seminal'." Another thing I want them to get into the habit of doing is looking up words they don't know the meanings of.

*   *   *

This assignment, like the next on Benjamin Franklin, is an example of learning as a process. I hope that it will give both us and the students a chance to elaborate on the connection of learning to language by raising the question of approach to result. Here is Malcolm X in prison, barely literate, copying out (and reading aloud what he had copied) the entire dictionary by hand. Here is Franklin with a scheme for self-improvement, a set of virtues and a checklist with which he rates himself at the end of each day. This is just rote learning from one point of view, but the question I want to focus on with these assignments is that of the relationship between what Malcolm X and Franklin told themselves that their rote learning meant and what they learned, what they became.

I believe that Malcolm X copied out the dictionary just as he says he did, because to have known enough to lie about such an experience was to have known enough to tell a better lie than he does—whatever impression he was trying to give of himself (the level of his prose does not, for me, argue the kind of sophistication that might have imagined that this is just what a reader *would* conclude). He did not, I think, know enough jargon about the learning process to know that he wasn't *supposed* to be able to learn from what he was doing. (I remember John Clark's suggesting once that the reason Chaucer was able to learn enough Italian in a few weeks to read Dante, and to be so influenced by what he had read as to be able to imitate it in *The House of Fame*, was that no one had ever told him learning a language that quickly and that well was impossible.) In other words, by copying out the dictionary (and reading aloud to himself what he had copied "over and over") Malcolm X grew because he wanted to and because he believed that he could; his copying and reading aloud was both the way he enacted his faith in the process of growth and the means by which he became more than he was. What he wanted was not words, an "education" in the sterile sense of the term, but an identity, to become someone with words. This is why all he knew about what he wanted to sound like was what he *didn't* want to sound like, a slob, everyone else, a Themewriter ("Look, daddy, let me pull your coat about a cat"). Malcolm X knew, that is, what we would have our students know by having them listen to themselves. He knew that to sound like nothing was to risk being nothing; he wanted language to enable him to change the plane on which he was living his life.

What Malcolm X did, then, was to develop a language which, in combining a way of expressing where he was with somewhere that he wanted to be, assured at least that he would grow. Hence "dictionary" for Malcolm X was not just something in which you look up words you don't know; it was an avenue to power, a road to becoming. "Words" were not just things made of letters, but the tools for forging an identity. Although Malcolm X undoubtedly could see his handwriting becoming better and his ability with words increasing, maybe he never became the writer and the speaker he wanted to become (who does?). But from another point of view maybe there is a way in which Malcolm X can be said to have done better than that. In his *attempt* to become more than he was, he developed a language that enabled him to belong to himself, to assume responsibility for the shape of his own life. He rote-learned what we would have our students rote-learn: that control of who one is in the act of becoming can be seen as a matter of language, and that language is a matter of choice.

12. Benjamin Franklin (Part I)

In his *Autobiography*, Benjamin Franklin tells of his dropping formal attendance at the Presbyterian church. He was in his mid-twenties at the time and had been what might be called today a "good Presbyterian" for most of his life. But he had been growing increasingly dissatisfied with not receiving from the Sunday services "the kind of good things that [he] expected." He was particularly disappointed in the sermons he heard, which he describes as "chiefly either polemic arguments or explications of the peculiar doctrines of our sect. To me [they were] very dry, uninteresting, and unedifying, since not a single moral principle was inculcated or enforced, their aim seeming to be rather to make us Presbyterians than good citizens."

Such windy Sundays came once too often, and though Franklin continued throughout his life to support the church as an institution by paying his annual subscription (he also made donations for the founding of other churches), he "went no more to the public assemblies." Franklin continues:

> It was about this time [that] I conceived the bold and arduous project of arriving at moral perfection. I wished to live without committing any fault at any time; I would conquer all that either natural inclination, custom, or company might lead me into. As I knew, or thought I knew, what was right and wrong, I did not see why I might not always do the one and avoid the other. But I soon found I had undertaken a task of more difficulty than I had imagined. While my care was employed in guarding against one fault, I was often surprised by another; habit took the advantage of inattention; inclination was sometimes too strong for reason. I concluded, at length, that the mere speculative conviction that it was to our interest to be completely virtuous, was not sufficient to prevent our slipping; and that the contrary habits must be broken, and good ones acquired and established, before we can have any dependence on a steady, uniform rectitude of conduct. For this purpose I therefore contrived the following method.
>
> In the various enumerations of the moral virtues I had met with in my reading, I found the catalogue more or less numerous, as different writers included more or fewer ideas under the same name. Temperance, for example, was by some confined to eating and drinking, while by others it was extended to mean the moderating of every other pleasure, appetite, inclination or passion, bodily or mental, even to our avarice and ambition. I proposed to myself

for the sake of clearness, to use rather more names, with fewer ideas annexed to each, than a few names with more ideas; and I included under thirteen names of virtues all that at that time occurred to me as necessary or desirable, and annexed to each a short precept, which fully expressed the extent I gave to its meaning.

These names of virtues, with their precepts, were:

1. *Temperance*—Eat not to dullness; drink not to elevation.
2. *Silence*—Speak not but what may benefit others or yourself; avoid trifling conversation.
3. *Order*—Let all your things have their places; let each part of your business have its time.
4. *Resolution*—Resolve to perform what you ought; perform without fail what you resolve.
5. *Frugality*—Make no expense but to do good to others or yourself; i.e., waste nothing.
6. *Industry*—Lose no time; be always employed in something useful; cut off all unnecessary actions.
7. *Sincerity*—Use no hurtful deceit; think innocently and justly, and if you speak, speak accordingly.
8. *Justice*—Wrong none by doing injuries, or omitting the benefits that are your duty.
9. *Moderation*—Avoid extremes; forbear resenting injuries so much as you think they deserve.
10. *Cleanliness*—Tolerate no uncleanliness in body, clothes, or habitation.
11. *Tranquility*—Be not disturbed at trifles, or at accidents common or unavoidable.
12. *Chastity*—Rarely use venery but for health or offspring, never to dullness, weakness, or the injury of your own or another's peace or reputation.
13. *Humility*—Imitate Jesus and Socrates.

My intention being to acquire the *habitude* of all these virtues, I judged it would be well not to distract my attention by attempting the whole at once, but to fix it on one of them at a time; and, when I should be master of that, then to proceed to another, and so on, till I should have gone through the thirteen; and, as the previous acquisition of some might facilitate the acquisition of certain others, I arranged them with that view, as they stand above. Temperance first, as it tends to procure that coolness and clearness of head, which is so necessary where constant vigilance was to be kept up, and guard maintained against the unremitting attraction of ancient habits, and the force of perpetual temptations. This being acquired and established *Silence* would be more easy; and my desire being to gain knowledge at the same time that I improved in virtue, and considering that in conversation it was obtained rather by the use of the ears than of the tongue, and therefore wishing to break a habit I was getting into of prattling, punning, and joking, which only made me acceptable to trifling company, I gave *Silence* the second place. This and the next, *Order,* I expected would allow me more time for attending to my project and my studies. *Resolution,* once become habitual, would keep me firm in my endeavors to obtain all the subsequent virtues; *Frugality* and *Industry* freeing me from my remaining debt, and producing affluence and independence, would make more easy the practice of *Sincerity* and *Justice,* etc., etc. Conceiving then, that, agreeably to the advice of Pythagoras in his Golden Verses, daily examination would be necessary, I contrived the following method for conducting that examination.

I made a little book, in which I allotted a page for each of the virtues. I ruled each page with red ink, so as to have seven columns, one for each day of the week, marking each column with a letter for the day. I crossed these columns with thirteen red lines, marking the beginning of each line with the first letter of one of the virtues, on which line, and in its proper column, I might mark, by a little black spot, every fault I found upon examination to have been committed respecting that virtue upon that day.

I determined to give a week's strict attention to each of the virtues successively. Thus, in the first week, my great guard was to avoid every day the least offence against *Temperance,* leaving the other virtues to their ordinary chance, only marking every evening the faults of the day. Thus, if in the first week I could keep my first line, marked T, clear of spots, I supposed the habit of that virtue so much strengthened, and its opposite weakened, that I might venture extending my attention to include the next, and for the following week keep both lines clear of spots. Proceeding thus to the last, I could go through a course complete in thirteen weeks, and four courses in a year. And like him who, having a garden to weed, does not attempt to eradicate all the bad herbs at once, which would exceed his reach and his strength, but works on one of the beds at a time, and, having accomplished the first, proceeds to a second, so I should have, I hoped, the encouraging pleasure of seeing on my pages the progress I made in virtue, by clearing successively my lines of their spots, till in the end, by a number of courses, I should be happy in viewing a clean book, after a thirteen weeks' daily examination.

—Benjamin Franklin *

* From *The Autobiography of Benjamin Franklin,* The Pocket Library, 1954, pp. 102–105.

The section of the *Autobiography* that we are concerned with here was written in 1784. Franklin was 79.

* * *

Franklin's scheme for self-development is based on certain assumptions about how he works as a human being, about the nature of human character. What are these assumptions? What is it he thought he could learn? What does he seem to think he can know?

Evidently, Franklin left off attending church less in anger than with a sense of disappointment. In what exactly? What did Franklin seem to think that a church should do? What does he mean, for example, by implying that moral principles should be both "inculcated" and "enforced?" What does he mean by a term such as "good citizens"?

Look over the list of virtues and their definitions. Reread what Franklin says about how he constructed it. Do you really think he did all that reading, all that selecting and modifying? What makes you say so?

What do you make of those virtues and their definitions? Are these just Pieties? Abstractions? Or can you infer anything more particular from them about the sort of man Franklin was? Perhaps it might help here for you to imagine what a list for yourself would look like.

Franklin explains why he arranged the virtues in the order he did. What do you understand from this explanation? Is there anything you do not understand from it?

The method Franklin contrived for conducting his daily examination involved him in the specific activity of making marks on paper (a form of writing?). Does this strike you as carrying things a bit too far? Couldn't he have kept score in his head, for example? Why do you suppose that Franklin seemed to think this specific daily activity was necessary?

Franklin says that in working at his project he was surprised to find himself "fuller of faults" than he imagined (what with all his markings and erasures, for example, he wore out that first "little book" and had to make himself another—with leaves of vellum the second time, not paper). But he goes on to say that he had "the satisfaction of seeing [his faults] diminish." Do you believe this?

Who would be the ideal audience for Benjamin Franklin? Characterize this audience as completely as you can.

Once again, examine the issues here in the light of your own life and experience. Have you ever set a project for yourself of the sort that Franklin did? Did the possibility ever occur to you? How do you account for the fact that it did or didn't? Does Franklin's project have anything to offer you? And how do you know? Be sure you explain what you mean by "project" here.

*   *   *

N.B.   Again, it is assumed that you will know something of the life and character of Benjamin Franklin when you come to class and that you will be able to supply written sources for your information.

13. *Benjamin Franklin (Part II)*

Franklin follows the account of his scheme of self-development with the following:

> It may be well my posterity should be informed that to this little artifice, with the blessing of God, their ancestor owed the constant felicity of his life, down to his 79th year, in which this is written. What reverses may attend the remainder is in the hand of Providence; but, if they arrive, the reflection on past happiness enjoyed ought to help his bearing them with more resignation. To Temperance he ascribes his long-continued health, and what is still left to him of a good constitution; to Industry and Frugality, the early easiness of his circumstances and acquisition of his fortune, with all that knowledge that enabled him to be a useful citizen, and obtained for him some degree of reputation among the learned; to Sincerity and Justice, the confidence of his country: and the honorable employs it conferred upon him; and to the joint influence of the whole mass of the virtues, even in the imperfect state he was able to acquire them, all that evenness of temper, and that cheerfulness in conversation, which makes his company still sought for, and agreeable even to his younger acquaintance. I hope, therefore, that some of my descendants may follow the example and reap the benefits.

> —*Benjamin Franklin* *

What do you make of such a way of talking, all those capital letters, for example; that pronoun shift ("my posterity"; "his 79th year") and back again ("I hope")?

When you compare the benefits which Franklin "ascribes" to his virtues above with the way he defines those same virtues in his original list, how would you describe the difference between what he seems to have hoped he would get from working on them and what he seems to have got?

How do you characterize the voice you hear speaking to you in the passage? What sort of tone does it have?

Are you being asked something in such a passage? Told something? Taught something? Or what exactly? And what is your response to what you hear?

* Ibid., p. 111.

Return to the question of whether or not you believe that Franklin saw his faults "diminish." Does the passage above influence your belief one way or another? Why?

Return also to the question of whether Franklin's project has anything to offer you. Is your stand on such a question the same as it was? How do you account for this? Do you understand the term "project" the way you first did? Why?

Commentary

Again, I will begin class with a brief quiz on Benjamin Franklin ("Franklin was the only American to have signed all three pieces of legislation establishing the United States as a nation: what were they?") and include in it some questions on the vocabulary of the assignment (define "inculcated"). I will also tell the students to prepare Assignment 13 for discussion next period. The day we take up Assignment 13 in class, I'll have the students prepare Assignments 14 (which is for class discussion) and 15 (for which I'll have the students write a paper) both for the following period.

*   *   *

In spite of the work we have done so far on the nature of rote learning, I think our students are going to find Franklin, and his plan for self-improvement, noxious. I think we will hear on the one hand that he is "stuffy" or "conceited," and on the other that he is a clock-work lemon, the original mechanical man, someone who thinks that human beings are "just computers," and so on. From another perspective, however, it seems to me that the mechanics of Franklin's scheme are a way of acknowledging the fact that the human spirit is anything but mechanical, and that in this sense both his scheme and the pride he takes in what it made possible are a great testament to the mysteriousness of human nature. At least this is the argument with which I am going to try to confront what I imagine will be the students' easy write-off of Franklin as sterile, his scheme as stillborn, and his attitudes as smug.

What I think students will have trouble seeing about Franklin's plan, first of all, is that it is a plan, a program for action and not some kind of Procrustean bed (it's "eat not to dullness," not "stay on 1000 calories a day"). Second, I think a lot of students are going to have difficulty understanding that Franklin's plan is a plan for Franklin, not a blueprint for the conduct of Everyman, and that as a plan it is carefully wrought in consideration of his own character (the importance of which Franklin suggests in the humorous way he dismisses his first [planless] aspiration "to live without committing any fault at any time"). That he did not do the reading that he says he did, for example, the selecting and the modifying, to me is inconceivable in the light of a definition of Frugality which reminds him to "make no expense but to do good to others or *yourself*" (my italics). Similiarly, would not a number of us, if we were applying the list to ourselves, find some conspicuous absences? Why did Franklin not list "Bravery," for example ("Remember to speak only what you think, not what you think others expect you to say"), or "Cheerfulness"? Obviously, Franklin did not consider a tendency to become depressed a problem. And the order of the virtues: which one of us would begin where Franklin does, with Temperance as his number one concern? I understand Franklin's explanation of the order of his virtues, of course, but I do not understand what that explanation explains. For the terms of his list are no more than a vocabulary which argues the existence of a syntax that is Benjamin Franklin himself, a syntax without which those terms are meaningless. Franklin's scheme *looks* abstract, *looks* like a blueprint, *looks* like something other than the highly individual, deeply personal construction it is only when I let my assumptions about the learning process, about what I think I can learn and how I think I have to learn it, blind me to the potential of my own development.

Like Malcolm X, Franklin too developed a language (his "writing" down every night his performance of the day) which in combining a way of expressing where he was (the check marks) with where he wanted to be (the frame that contained the check marks) assured at least that he would grow. Also like Malcolm X, Franklin in a way did better than become what he had set out to become. He saw his faults "diminish," but by his own admission he never attained the perfection he hoped for. Yet in the attempt to become more than he was, Franklin too seems to have developed a language that enabled him to belong to himself, that brought him something different from, and finally more than, what he had sought (hence his attributing to his virtues benefits that go far beyond anything he had been able to imagine would be the result of his efforts to observe them: "to Industry and Frugality [he owes] the early easiness of his circumstances and the acquisition of his fortune"). Franklin, too, developed a way of assuming responsibility for, and hence control of, the direction of his life.

What Franklin offers his "descendents," readers, then, is not *his* plan, but an example of what *a* plan can accomplish: "to this little artifice, with the blessing of God, their ancestor owed the constant felicity of his life." He offers, that is, his life and its accomplishments, himself, not as what resulted from his own efforts (even though it did), but as what resulted from the power of a mere contrivance, a mere contrivance to which he nevertheless owes everything. "Look," it is as though Franklin were saying, "if this scheme, which is not so much, did all this for me, then does not that argue the value of your developing a scheme for yourself, for your life, which can do something similar for you?" Franklin offers the value of behaving as though one believed it were possible to become a better person. He offers mechanics in the name and for the sake of what is much more than mechanical.

Thus Franklin does not seem to have left the church in anger, or because he believed that it had no answers for anyone. He left it because it had no answers for him, no answers he could use. Franklin left the church in order to create what would make him a "good citizen," a whole man, a man for whom theology was morality and morality the unabstract stuff of his daily living. He left the church, so far as I'm concerned, in order to create one, and ended up becoming created by what he sought to create (hence his ability to see himself as an "I" and as a "he" simultaneously). No wonder Franklin looks on his virtues almost as though they were people, almost as though they were friends ("all those capital letters"). No wonder he sees his success as a gift. The voice I hear in the paragraph quoted in Assignment 13 is one of reverence, a peculiar blend of pride and of humility. It is the voice of a man conscious of himself as an institution, but a man conscious also that he has been made an institution by something bigger than he is to which he remains profoundly grateful.

14. D. H. Lawrence

D. H. Lawrence in his *Studies in Classic American Literature* devotes a chapter to Benjamin Franklin and has this to say about his scheme of self-development:

> I am a moral animal. But I am not a moral machine. I don't work with a little set of handles or levers. The temperance-silence-order - resolution - frugality - industry - sincerity - justice - moderation - cleanliness-tranquillity-chastity-humility keyboard is not going to get me going. I'm really not just an automatic piano with a moral Benjamin getting tunes out of me.*

And then Lawrence, too, develops a list:

1. *Temperance*—Eat and carouse with Bacchus, or munch dry bread with Jesus, but don't sit down without one of the gods.
2. *Silence*—Be still when you have nothing to say; when genuine passion moves you, say what you've got to say, and say it hot.
3. *Order*—Know that you are responsible to the gods inside you and to the men in whom the gods are manifest. Recognize your superiors and your inferiors, according to the gods. This is the root of all order.
4. *Resolution*—Resolve to abide by your own deepest promptings, and to sacrifice the smaller thing to the greater. Kill when you must, and be killed the same: the must coming from the gods inside you, or from the men in whom you recognize the Holy Ghost.
5. *Frugality*—Demand nothing; accept what you see fit. Don't waste your pride or squander your emotion.
6. *Industry*—Lose no time with ideals; serve the Holy Ghost; never serve mankind.
7. *Sincerity*—To be sincere is to remember that I am I, and that the other man is not me.
8. *Justice*—The only justice is to follow the sincere intuition of the soul, angry or gentle. Anger is just, and pity is just, but judgment is never just.
9. *Moderation*—Beware of absolutes. There are many gods.
10. *Cleanliness*—Don't be too clean. It impoverishes the blood.

* From *Studies in Classic American Literature* by D. H. Lawrence. Copyright © 1923, 1951 by Frieda Lawrence, © 1961 by the Estate of the late Frieda Lawrence. Reprinted by permission of The Viking Press, Inc.

11. *Tranquility*—The soul has many motions, many gods come and go. Try and find your deepest issue, in every confusion, and abide by that. Obey the man in whom you recognize the Holy Ghost; command when your honour comes to command.

12. *Chastity*—Never "use" venery at all. Follow your passional impulse, if it be answered in the other being; but never have any motive in mind, neither offspring nor health nor even pleasure, nor even service. Only know that "venery" is of the great gods. An offering-up of yourself to the very great gods, the dark ones, and nothing else.

13. *Humility*—See all men and women according to the Holy Ghost that is within them. Never yield before the barren.

There's my list. I have been trying dimly to realize it for a long time, and only America and old Benjamin have at last goaded me into trying to formulate it. And now I, at least, know why I can't stand Benjamin. He tries to take away my wholeness and my dark forest, my freedom. For how can any man be free, without an illimitable background? And Benjamin tries to shove me into a barbed wire paddock and make me grow potatoes or Chicagoes.

And how can I be free, without gods that come and go? But Benjamin won't let anything exist except my useful fellow men, and I'm sick of them; as for his Godhead, his Providence, He is Head of nothing except a vast heavenly store that keeps every imaginable line of goods, from victrolas to cat-o'-nine tails.

*　　*　　*

Lawrence's essay on Franklin is also predicated on certain assumptions about what it means to be a human being, about what is learnable, what is knowable. Trace out these assumptions. How do they compare with what you see as Franklin's assumptions about the way in which people are people? The following are for the purpose of helping you to locate yourself with these questions.

Look over Lawrence's list of virtues. What do you make of his definitions of Franklin's terms? Are these definitions clear? Do you understand, for example, what Lawrence means by "the gods" (of whom Bacchus and Jesus seem to be two)? How about "the Holy Ghost"? You have, presumably, seen such terms before.

Lawrence also makes use of terms for which you may have no immediate context: "the dark ones," "my dark forest." What do you make of them?

If you find yourself unable to supply equivalents for some of Lawrence's terms, if you cannot translate into your own language the concept of sexuality, say, that seems to underlie what Lawrence says of *Chastity,* then does that mean that you have no idea of what he is talking about? Would you feel right saying that Lawrence is simply incomprehensible? Or can you, out of the corner of your eye, see the possibility of another way of talking here?

What do you think Lawrence is doing in his essay on Franklin? Is he attacking him? Is he trying to teach something? Who would make up the ideal audience for D. H. Lawrence?

Does Lawrence have anything to offer you? Are his assumptions about the nature of human character your assumptions? Or do you disagree with him? Are you comfortable in your agreement or disagreement? Why?

* * *

N.B. Once more, as you found out about Malcolm X and Benjamin Franklin, find out about D. H. Lawrence by the time you come to class.

Commentary

I'll begin class by collecting the papers addressed to Assignment 15 (which we'll take up in the usual way the next period) and then, again, I'll give the students a five minute quiz ("Name two novels written by D. H. Lawrence," etc.).

* * *

Since "what it means to be a human being," the nature of human nature, is less an "it" than a construct one makes on the basis of his assumptions about (among other things) what is learnable, what is knowable, it is of course possible to develop a model for human character that is different from Franklin's. It is not important whether the students "agree" with Lawrence's assumptions about the nature of human character (or for that matter with Franklin's), but it is important that they realize that the validity of seeing it one way (any way) as opposed to seeing it another has less to do with the nature of "being" in some abstract sense than with what one decides his responsibilities as a person are going to be on the basis of how he chooses to see it. It is this notion that I see the assignment on D. H. Lawrence giving us the chance to make available.

The manner of Lawrence's essay makes it difficult to determine what he really thought that Franklin assumed about the nature of human character, for Lawrence is much less interested in Franklin than he is in using Franklin's rhetoric as the occasion for establishing a relationship with his reader—or more accurately, for dramatizing to a reader a relationship he has with himself. (If you like Lawrence, as I do, you say that the intention of this self-dramatization is to make a reader question the nature of the relationship he has with himself in order to enable him to work out a better one; if you do not like Lawrence, you say that his intention is to rouse a reader's envy in such a way as to compel him to an emulation which can result in nothing but frustration.) Franklin's use of such terms as "habit and inclination" and the celebrative wonderment of his tone in the paragraph we use as the basis of Assignment 13 suggest to me that he was well aware that human nature was anything but knowable in the final sense. His emphasis is upon dealing with human character in such a way as to make its mysteriousness irrelevant to what one does to improve it, which is quite a different thing from suggesting that there is no mystery to human nature at all. But I would be uncomfortable asserting that this is a distinction that Lawrence was unaware of. He was too good a reader for one thing. For another, as I have already suggested, he was interested in something other than Being Fair to Franklin. The charge of unfairness, the idea that Lawrence is "attacking" Franklin, strikes me as less wrong than irrelevant.

It's that display of spiritual fireworks in Lawrence's prose that has my attention as a reader, the effects he generates out of making Franklin stand for a mechanical approach to human development and human relations (and therefore a limiting notion of human nature) against which he is then able to play his sense of human nature as darkly and richly illimitable, as mysterious—mysterious, that is, for everyone but Lawrence. For the success of Lawrence's prose here lies in the writer's ability to create the illusion that his speaker is at one with, that he knows or is a part of, something tremendously important to know about human nature, something that I as a reader seem to have some dim (almost remembered) awareness of, but lack the power to articulate or use. This effect Lawrence achieves partly through the declamatory certainty of his tone (his ability to fuse the formal and the pious with the colloquial and the humorous in such a way as to suggest that no amalgamation is beyond him) and partly through the way he orchestrates his metaphors. I am clear, for example, that "Jesus," "Bacchus," and "Holy Ghost" are being used metaphorically (there is no traditional theology in which Jesus and Bacchus are part of the same pantheon; the injunction to kill is not ordinarily associated with the Christian Holy Ghost), but I am not at all clear what it is that as metaphors they designate—particularly when they are coupled as they are with other metaphors, those for which I have no immediate correlatives ("the gods," "the dark ones"). I find my position even more frustrating because Lawrence's placing of both sorts of metaphors suggests a meaning for them that I seem somehow to know about, or that perhaps I once knew about, or maybe that I can know about if only I am—attentive enough? honest enough? courageous enough? It is an effect like the effect of nonsense in which things seem to go together, but in a way that cannot quite be grasped. And yet the effect is not like that of nonsense, because I am never released enough to be able to say, "This cannot be worked out." The most I can say as a reader is, "I cannot work it out." The possibility remains that it *can* be worked out. And that it has been. By Lawrence.

It is this quality of Lawrence's prose that makes either agreeing or disagreeing with what seems to be his conception of the nature of human character equally disquieting. To write off his tone as rant, his manner as excessive or bad-tempered, his matter as private theosophy, is to murder one's sense of the sound of importance in what is being talked about (which a reader has to become engaged with in order to read the passage at all)—a murder which one cannot escape the possibility is perhaps a murder of one's self as well, his own potential for growth and change. On the other hand, to agree with Lawrence on the nature of human character (and by more than implication to a way of behaving as well: Lawrence's list is far more injunctive than Franklin's), in addition to raising the difficulty of knowing exactly what it is that one has agreed to, raises also the specter of one's possible spiritual inferiority. Am I really capable of serving *this* Holy Ghost in myself, the suspicion runs, or in others? How do I distinguish the injunctions of a "god" from those of a devil, or "genuine passion" from what is only a shadow of the real thing? Even if I could tell my "passional impulse" from motived sexual desire (and who does not have the illusion that there is such a distinction to be made, and that he, at least sometimes, may be capable of making it?)—could I "follow" it, wherever it led?

I am not, of course, going to get into all of this with the students in just these terms. In spite of our questions about Lawrence, I think that what the students will read, understand, take a position on is not what Lawrence is saying, not what his language is saying, but what they will reduce him and his language to meaning with their conventional (rote-learned) associations with such terms as "Holy Ghost," "dark," "gods," "passion," and the rest. They will not, that is, understand that Lawrence is playing off against one another the conventional associations we have with such terms in order to create a conception of character quite different from that assumed by conventional Christianity or by any convention that they can name. They will not understand that the only dictionary that will define such terms is Lawrence's syntax for them, the metaphoric structures that they both create and are created by. Finally, I do not expect the students to understand by themselves that Lawrence's attempt to define human character as he does, by triangulating rather than stating it, is a way of saying that character, being, cannot be defined as a thing, cannot be explained in such a way as to be grasped. They will not, in other words, know that they cannot name what Lawrence's syntax defines as unnameable, that the whole effect of his language is to create, to evoke, a sense of that which cannot *be* defined. Hence I expect we will have Lawrence offered to us as "deeply religious," as a spokesman for "naturalness," as someone who believed people ought to "follow their own impulses," be more "free" or "relaxed," and so on. I intend to complicate such responses in the same way I did their responses to Franklin: "Can you show me how 'Holy Ghost' means what you say it does in this context?" (moving from 6 to 13, back to 4); "If Lawrence is, as you say, telling you to do your own thing, can you tell me how you understand what he says under 3?"; "How are you 'free' when you are told to 'obey the man in whom you recognize the Holy Ghost'?"

As I've said, I don't care whether the students "agree" with Lawrence or not, but I want to conclude the period by asking what kind of responsibility for one's life (and how much) Lawrence's assumptions about the nature of human character would seem to allow for.

15. *The Perfect Student*

This diagram of the Perfect Student was constructed by a teacher of composition who was annoyed with the way in which his students chose to describe themselves. (Annoyed with what, do you suppose?)

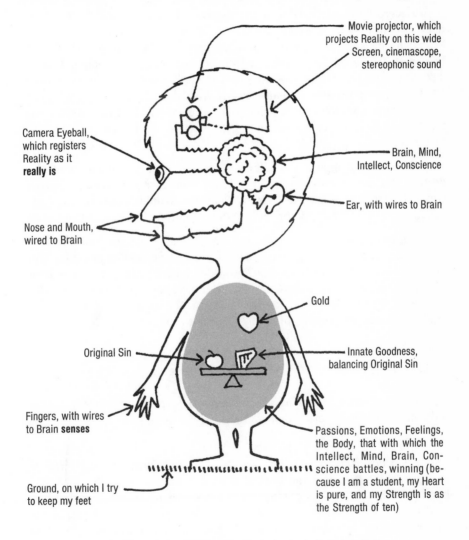

Diagram of the Perfect Student (After a diagram by John F. Butler)

It is really a diagram of a number of commonly used metaphors placed within a simple plan of the human body. The result is laughable, yet there is some meaning conveyed by the diagram which we can recognize. We do speak of someone's heart of gold and we do describe the nervous system as if it were an electronic device. That is, under certain circumstances we are inclined to talk this way.

*   *   *

According to the details of the diagram, how does this Perfect Student operate? How does he go about learning? What can he know? Would he be able to copy out the dictionary as Malcolm X did? Could he construct and follow a project of the sort devised by Benjamin Franklin? Would he be able to look at Franklin's scheme for self-improvement as D. H. Lawrence did? Perhaps, and if you'd like equal time, you could address these questions by devising a diagram of the Perfect Teacher for this Perfect Student, or by attempting to imagine the Perfect Educational Institution for him.

When you compare yourself as a student with this diagram of the Perfect Student, what do you find? Have you ever behaved as though you believed you were the Perfect Student? Would there be any advantages to someone's doing so? Would there be any disadvantages?

But of course you are not the Perfect Student. How are you different? Is it going to be enough to claim, as the Perfect Student might, that you think, or that you are an Individual? How do you see yourself as the student you think you are? What metaphors do you have for how you operate, for what you want to learn, to know? Are you not as good as the Perfect Student? Better off? Simply different? Or what, exactly?

Commentary

I'll begin class by asking the students to prepare Assignment 16 for a discussion the next period that we meet.

*   *   *

I will not expect most of my students to have much difficulty recognizing in the diagram of the Perfect Student a comment on the way they began the course by describing themselves. There is nothing that my students in their first few papers claimed to do or to want or to care about that is beyond the operation of the Perfect Student. The Perfect Student writes Perfect English Papers. The Perfect Student is the Themewriter. He is everything except an individual with an individual voice.

But we are asking the students to do more on this assignment than simply to say What Fools They Were, or are prone to be—Perfect Student self-recrimination, Themetalk about the Themewriter. We are asking them to take responsibility for what they are likely to have done or to do by seeing this assignment as an opportunity to do something else. "Here," we are saying, "in this diagram is a comment on the box that you are likely to have nailed yourself into on the basis of how you have had a tendency to represent yourself in your writing. If you don't like being in this box, then you've got to write yourself out of it. Now, how are you going to do that? How are you going to represent yourself some other way?"

I think we had better be ready to expect that for some students this other way will not really be another way at all. I will be surprised, that is, if I do not have students who will find the diagram inadequate for no better reason than that it is incomplete, insufficiently detailed in its mechanical operations ("My brain is more complex than this" or "There's no sorter-outer here" or "There's no putter-togetherer"). But I hope I will have more than just one or two students who will follow the drift of our questions well enough to question the conception of the diagram in its totality to account for a person as a totality (whose mind and feelings interact), who will see that it is *their* complexity, *their* sorting out or putting together expressed as an action of their *own,* that that diagram, that no diagram, could get them to.

The "metaphors" our students develop for how they do operate will be the papers that they write, and as I hope is apparent from the various ways in which we invite them to deal with the subject, there is no one way we can expect they will proceed with it. I can imagine a student's doing a diagram of a Perfect Teacher for this Perfect Student, for example, which would display his awareness of the Perfect Student's mechanical nature through a representation of the Teacher as an impossible multiplicity: the Prophet-Seer who can instantly become Mommy. Or perhaps we will have the Perfect Educational Institution designed as an elaborate vending machine. Or I can imagine someone's spending all of his paper on a comparison of the Perfect Student with Malcolm X or Franklin or Lawrence (and finding, perhaps, that the Perfect Student could never even have got so far as to copy out the dictionary in the way that Malcolm X did because, since he looks on Reality as it *really is,* he could never have seen the dictionary as anything other than something in which to look up words). I can even imagine a fine paper's being done on no more than how a given student sees himself as sometimes operating in just the way the Perfect Student does, knowing rather than learning, wanting the Answer rather than an answer for himself. The key question of the assignment for me is going to be the question of the final paragraph: "How do you see yourself as the student you think you are?" Any attempt by anyone to enact the operations of this "you" in the form of a set of sentences about which a *reader* can say, "Yes, he is an individual," I will praise beyond measure.

16. S. H. Hadley

Here is another account of what can be seen as a learning experience:

One Tuesday evening I sat in a saloon in Harlem, a homeless, friendless, dying drunkard. I had pawned or sold everything that would bring a drink. I could not sleep unless I was dead drunk. I had not eaten for days, and for four nights preceding I had suffered with delirium tremens, or the horrors, from midnight till morning. I had often said, "I will never be a tramp. I will never be cornered, for when that time comes, if ever it comes, I will find a home in the bottom of the river." But the Lord so ordered it that when that time did come I was not able to walk one quarter of the way to the river. As I sat there thinking, I seemed to feel some great and mighty presence. I did not know then what it was. I did learn afterwards that it was Jesus, the sinner's friend. I walked up to the bar and pounded it with my fist till I made the glasses rattle. Those who stood by drinking looked on with scornful curiosity. I said I would never take another drink, if I died on the street, and really I felt as though that would happen before morning. Something said, "If you want to keep this promise, go and have yourself locked up." I went to the nearest station-house and had myself locked up.

I was placed in a narrow cell, and it seemed as though all the demons that could find room came in that place with me. This was not all the company I had, either. No, praise the Lord; that dear Spirit that came to me in the saloon was present, and said, Pray. I did pray, and though I did not feel any great help, I kept on praying. As soon as I was able to leave my cell I was taken to the police court and remanded back to the cell. I was finally released, and found my way to my brother's house, where every care was given me. While lying in bed the admonishing Spirit never left me, and when I arose the following Sabbath morning I felt that day would decide my fate, and toward evening it came into my head to go to Jerry M'Auley's Mission. I went. The house was packed, and with great difficulty I made my way to the space near the platform. There I saw the apostle to the drunkard and the outcast —that man of God, Jerry M'Auley. He rose, and amid deep silence told [of] his experience [as a drunkard and of his recovery from alcoholism through a belief in Christ]. There was a sincerity about this man that carried conviction with it, and I found myself saying, "I wonder if God can save me?" I listened to the testimony of twenty-five or thirty persons every one of whom had been saved from rum, and I made up my mind that I would be saved or die right there. When the invitation was given, I knelt down with a crowd of drunkards. Jerry made the first prayer. Then Mrs. M'Auley prayed fervently for us. Oh, what a conflict was going on for my poor soul! A blessed whisper said, "Come"; the devil said, "Be careful." I halted but a moment, and then, with a breaking heart, I said, "Dear Jesus, can you help me?" Never with mortal tongue can I describe that moment. Although up to that moment my soul had been filled with indescribable gloom, I felt the glorious brightness of the noonday sun shine into my heart. I felt I was a free man. Oh, the precious feeling of safety, of freedom, of resting on Jesus! I felt that Christ with all his brightness and power had come into my life; that, indeed, old things had passed away and all things had become new.

From that moment till now I have never wanted a drink of whiskey, and I have never seen money enough to make me take one. I promised God that night that if he would take away that appetite for strong drink, I would work for him all my life. He has done his part, and I have been trying to do mine.*

That Hadley was a drunkard who quite suddenly became sober and to the end of his life never touched alcohol again is a matter of record. William James, who quotes Hadley's account of himself in his *Varieties of Religious Experience,* says that after his conversion he became "an active and useful rescuer of [other] drunkards in New York."

This is an account of what is sometimes called a conversion experience. One state of mind or being is exchanged for another. To judge from what Hadley has written, where would you locate the moment of his change of mind, of his conversion? What brings the change about? What is this mind that Hadley changes? From what to what does he change it?

The following are intended to help you locate yourself in addressing these questions.

Hadley sees the talk of Jerry M'Auley as crucial to his change of mind, his conversion. Yet it is difficult to believe that Hadley had not heard of Jesus Christ before his meeting with M'Auley. Why do you think that M'Auley's talk seems to have made the difference to him that it did?

You will remember from your experience with Assignment 4 that once you change your mind it is hard to recall what your previous state of mind had been, what it was you changed from, how you could ever not know what is now so plain, how you could ever not see what is now right before your eyes. Does Hadley seem to have any difficulty recalling

* S. H. Hadley, *Rescue Mission Work,* Old Jerry M'Auley Water Street Mission, New York, 1890.

his previous state of mind? With what terminology does he organize his state of mind before his conversion, for example? Is there a difference between that terminology and the terminology with which he organizes his present? His future?

So far as Hadley's future is concerned, he did indeed become, as James says, "an active and useful rescuer of [other] drunkards." Like M'Auley, his way of becoming active was to tell his own story. At mission meeting after mission meeting he repeated it and repeated it and repeated it. (Perhaps, as Malcolm X seems to have been, Hadley was ignorant of what has happened in the world since 1872 or thereabouts?) Whatever effect this activity of Hadley's may have had on others, what effect do you imagine it might have had on him?

It would, of course, be possible for someone other than Hadley to explain what happened to him another way, with another set of terms. How might a Freudian explain Hadley's experience, for example? Or a Jungian? Or an atheist? How and for whom might the use of another set of terms for explaining Hadley's experience be beneficial? How and for whom might the same set of other terms be other than beneficial?

Hadley himself might have chosen to explain what happened to him another way, with another set of terms. Suppose, for example, he chose to call that "great and mighty presence" a hallucination? Suppose he had chosen to see what went on at M'Auley's as hokum? What differences, exactly, would such changes in terminology have made? Is not a rose a rose by any name?

"We learn from our experience." You are familiar with the proverbial connection. "Experience is the best teacher." But what kind of talk is this? You have for example, experienced the telephone dial in full detail and recently. But can you say for sure right now at what letter the lettering order on the dial reverses itself? (On the other hand, you might feel on safer ground with the little dot at the center of the dialing holes?) Similarly, when you notice the various ways in which what happened to Hadley can be talked about, does it seem accurate to say that it was from his *experience* that Hadley learned? What then did he learn from? What saved him from drink?

Commentary

I'll begin class by asking the students to prepare Assignment 17 for a discussion the next period that we meet and also to write a paper addressing Assignment 18 to be turned in that same period.

*　　*　　*

S. H. Hadley's account of himself verifies the validity of our insisting on the importance of language to the learning process by providing a very clear example of a man's making sense of his present with a language for his past that gives him a chance for a future.

Once it is recognized that what happened to Hadley could from another point of view very easily be explained with different terms (Freudian, Jungian, Skinnerian, etc.), it is clear that what "saved" him is language *about* an experience, not the experience itself (any more than the mere exposure of our students to the telephone dial enabled them to reproduce it from memory). What changed Hadley's life is how he *named* what happened to him.

Perhaps it is not accurate to say that without the language M'Auley gave him Hadley would have *had* no experience, but it is certainly demonstrable that he would not have had the experience he did. Before M'Auley offers Hadley the terms with which to make sense of his life (M'Auley and, presumably, the "twenty-five or thirty" others who evidently spoke of a "Jesus" in conjunction with "drunkenness" in such a way as to create for Hadley a new way of seeing old concepts, new definitions that implied a new language) the "great and mighty presence" of the saloon is as much a torment to Hadley as it is a comfort. It is a "something," a "dear Spirit" that enjoins him to prayer, but to prayer from which he feels no "great help." Later, at his brother's, the Spirit is "admonishing." Even at M'Auley's, Hadley's soul is "in conflict." It is not until the "something" is identified with "Jesus" (who is in turn defined as a power synonymous with protection, comfort, friendship, and salvation) that the present is made sense of with a language that enables Hadley to organize his past and future as well. Without Hadley's experience at M'Auley's (a wordless, languageless moment, by the way, as are all moments of a change of mind: "and then with a breaking heart"), would Hadley have been able to see himself as "a homeless, friendless, dying drunkard" in just those terms? Would he have been able to express what he felt in the bar as the presence of something "great and mighty" (which he learns "afterwards . . . was Jesus, the sinner's friend")? Would he have been able to see his cell as filled with "demons" opposed by a "dear Spirit"? Would he have been able to see his life as at one with "work for" God in the way that he does?

Another way of explaining what happened to Hadley ("his conscience began to bother him"; "he had hallucinations"; "he just got sick and tired of being sick and tired") would have, perhaps, the advantage of making his experience more accessible to others (which is why the spirituality of Alcoholics Anonymous, incidentally, is phrased in language that gives the widest possible latitude for interpretation: "God as we understand Him"—meaning as each individual understands Him for himself; "a Power greater than ourselves"—meaning anything anyone wants to call larger than he is); but a completely secularized interpretation of Hadley's experience would run the risk of being an interpretation robbed of transforming power. For what saved Hadley was a very particular language, a language which in enabling him to postulate a power greater than himself gave him a power greater than he had. (Almost certainly Hadley had heard the name "Jesus" before he met M'Auley, but he had never, presumably, heard it defined or been ready to hear it defined, as M'Auley defined it—in terms of its relation to his particular kind of dereliction.) Hadley's becoming "an active and useful rescuer of [other] drunkards" in the way that he evidently did (what else would he have become "active and useful" with if not the telling of his own story?) was how he made and kept that language his, the way he rote-learned where he never again had to be. How Hadley named is thereby a demonstrable reflex of what he was choosing to be. What Hadley came to learn was a set of terms that gave him control over his life. What caused him to *want* to learn what he did, there are millions of addicts for whose sake I wish I knew.

17. A Madman

The passage below is quoted by William James in a section of *Varieties of Religious Experience,* subtitled "The Sick Soul" (Modern Library Edition, pp. 145–146). It is a letter written by an inmate of a mental institution, a patient for whom James says "the sun has left his heaven" (p. 146). James's book (the full title of which is *The Varieties of Religious Experience: A Study in Human Nature*) was first published in 1902.

I suffer too much in this hospital, both physically and morally. Besides the burnings and the sleeplessness (for I no longer sleep since I am shut up here, and the little rest I get is broken by bad dreams, and I am waked with a jump by nightmares, dreadful visions, lightning, thunder, and the rest), fear, atrocious fear, presses me down, holds me without respite, never lets me go. Where is the justice in it all! What have I done to deserve this excess of severity? Under what form will this fear crush me? What would I not owe to any one who would rid me of my life! Eat, drink, lie awake all night, suffer without interruption—such is the fine legacy I have received from my mother! What I fail to understand is this abuse of power. There are limits to everything, there is a middle way. But God knows neither middle way nor limits. I say God, but why? All I have known so far has been the devil. After all, I am afraid of God as much as of the devil, so I drift along, thinking of nothing but suicide, but with neither courage nor means here to execute the act. As you read this, it will easily prove to you my insanity. The style and the ideas are incoherent enough—I can see that myself. But I cannot keep myself from being either crazy or an idiot; and, as things are, from whom should I ask pity? I am defenseless against the invisible enemy who is tightening his coils around me. I should be no better armed against him even if I saw him, or had seen him. Oh, if he would but kill me, devil take him! Death, death, once for all! But I stop. I have raved to you long enough. I say raved, for I can write no otherwise, having neither brain nor thoughts left. O God! what a misfortune to be born! Born like a mushroom, doubtless between an evening and a morning; and how true and right I was when in our philosophy-year in college I chewed the cud of bitterness with the pessimists. Yes, indeed, there is more pain in life than gladness—it is one long agony until the grave. Think how gay it makes me to remember that this horrible misery of mine, coupled with this unspeakable fear, may last fifty, one hundred, who knows how many more years!

First of all, the voice you hear speaking in the passage is not totally unfamiliar to you, is it? Not to you, not to anyone. Why? Where and under what circumstances have you heard something like that voice before? What is familiar about what you hear in the passage? But the way you hear that voice in other circumstances is not the way you hear it here. Why not?

Malcolm X, Franklin, D. H. Lawrence, and S. H. Hadley in their attempts to become more than they were, may all be said to have developed languages, or ways of seeing themselves and their experience, that enabled them to assume responsibility for the shapes of their own lives, to grow, to belong to themselves. To judge from what he has written, the writer of the passage above has also told himself about his experience in order to establish a relationship with it. What is this relationship exactly? With what terms does he organize the world he lives in? How does he define these terms? To what end is the process directed?

Project yourself into a position that it is no exaggeration to say you may someday find yourself in. Assume that the statement above represents a state of mind for which you have chosen to accept some reponsibility. How would you characterize the speaker of that passage for yourself? As mentally disturbed? As faking? Explain what you would mean by whatever terms you think you would choose. Do you think your choice of terms would make a difference?

What would you say or do in the face of this phenomenon that you have chosen to accept some responsibility for? Would you talk to the speaker? How? What would you say? Or would your talking do no good? Would talking itself do no good? What do you think would help the speaker of the passage? Jesus? (meaning what exactly?) Psychiatric Treatment? (which would involve?)

Commentary

I'll begin class by collecting the papers the students have written addressing Assignment 18 and have them write a paper addressing Assignment 19 to be turned in the following period.

*   *   *

The passage we are using for this assignment inverts the process we see at work in the passage by Hadley: language here is used not to order and make livable the chaos of experience but to turn experience into chaos which is unlivable. What makes the passage madness is the image it provides of someone's choosing to live the unlivable.

I do not know anyone to whom a moment of despair is unfamiliar, anyone who could look at the language of this poor wretch and say: "I have never felt that way." But because it is someones with whom most of us deal, people we see as people and not as non-people or mad, we are inclined at first to name the state of mind expressed by the letter with terminology that suggests we see it as a state of mind and not a state of being. "I'm depressed," I say, or "down," or "feeling blue," or "full of self-pity." But there is no doubleness in the letter that way, no self for which excessive pity is being felt, no language suggestive of a mind to which this feeling is merely momentary. The voice of the passage is one that can name anything, but which names in such a way as to assure that the self-control and self-location that ordinarily attends the act of naming results only in no-control, no-location, nothing. Hence anything which could carry the possibility of restoration or comfort—sleep, education, family, hospital, God, philosophy, even the saving distance that ordinarily attends the use of wit or irony ("think how gay it makes me")—is defined as its opposite, named (or used) in such a way as to bankrupt the whole activity of naming. Sleep becomes nightmare, hospital a place of suffering, to be born is a "misfortune," and so on. God becomes "the devil," which becomes "the invisible enemy," which is reduced further to a "him," and finally to an "it"—an "it" made coterminous with the "horrible misery" of consciousness itself. It is not a world such a voice creates but an anti-world, one in which Hadley's "mighty presence" and "admonishing spirit" moves, not to the saving formulation of a concept such as "Jesus," but back to the rawness of indefinable sensation. If Hadley found a language which became The Language for him, the madman is making use of what his manner asserts is The Language period, actuality itself, a way of talking which denies the possibility of all other ways of talking and yet which creates the opposite of creation. Even the madman's nominal recognition of this craziness is made in such a way as to confirm his commitment to it ("this . . . will easily prove to you my insanity"). He is his own sickness, as he must continue to be because the ferocity of his devotion to allowing no vantage point from which to develop a language for the placing of his sickness as sickness is his pledge to remain his own prisoner. (He has totally closed himself to all possibility of seeing, for example, that the horror of "the style and the ideas" of his letter is not that they are, as he says, "incoherent." The real horror is that they are perfectly coherent.)

For me to accept responsibility for such a person would be to have to admit that it was not a "person" I was dealing with. There are only two things I can imagine penetrating the madman's world. One is a language that I cannot conceive of (do psychiatrists have such a language?). The other (perhaps this is only the last statement phrased differently) is a stronger anti-language than the madman's (drugs, shock treatments), which could be used to destroy in him what now keeps language from being a possibility for him.

18. A Good Teacher

The evaluation of a teacher's effectiveness as a teacher is a complicated business. "Teacher" and "effective" mean different things to different people. The terms can also mean different things at different times to the same person. A generally agreed upon unit of measure, therefore, is difficult to come by. A standard scale is difficult to come by.

What is true for the evaluator of a teacher is no less true of the teacher himself. Every teacher does some things well and other things not so well. And like his students, every teacher has good days and bad days. Every teacher is a person as well as a teacher—with all that that implies.

Here, for example, is an account of a teacher by one of his former students:

Dr. Albert Thomas Carter died on 29th July. . . . He was 85; and was the most individual and pungent Tutor [1] in the House [2] from 1895 to 1923. To sum up his contradictions in proper perspective is not easy. With his long, lean, legal, Mephistophelian face and beautiful elocution, he was as memorable for his reading of the Lessons in Cathedral [3] as for his highly polished and often luridly startling stories, and for his well-known aphorisms: "live and let die"; "self not service"; "anything to give pain"; "the best is good enough for me." . . . His intellect was brilliant—cool, sharp, and ruthless; he had got Firsts in Mods and Greats, [4] the Eldon and the Vinerian, [5] and had lectured for long as Reader in Constitutional Law and Legal History at the Inns of Court: [6] and he was the author of two crisp and lucid legal books. For potential Firsts and Blues, [7] the common objects of academic snobbery in aging Tutors, he was a magnificent teacher; with idlers his methods could be the more horrifying for their inhuman and sardonic suavity; if they would

[1] In English universities, a college official in charge of the studies of an undergraduate.
[2] Christ Church, Oxford.
[3] Reading of scripture in chapel.
[4] Honors in intermediate examinations and classics.
[5] Endowed professorships.
[6] The four voluntary legal societies in England which have the exclusive right to call candidates to the English bar, after they have received such instruction and taken such examinations as the Inns stipulate and provide. A Reader is a lecturing professor.
[7] Honor students and varsity athletes.

not try, neither would he, except to make things unpleasant for them. He was by nature easily tolerant and benevolent, and to his friends a constant but anxious joy, and he won their real affection. But to the dim and weakly he could be unpardonably and odiously cruel, and he was irascible at games. When Albany [8] was bombed, he moved for a time to Queen's, his old College, which had made him an Honorary Fellow; he didn't mind danger in London, he said, but could not bear discomfort. But he was a highly critical and unaccommodating war-time lodger, and at last returned to Albany and to a sadly solitary existence made worse by failing sight. His collection of silver was superb; and when to add to it became too costly even for him, he made a splendid collection of English gold coins, which he said were cheaper. . . . To cheerful youth, as he loved to call it, "The Don" was a great figure; his entertainments were memorable; and he was worldly wise to a degree unusual in dons. Friendly, ribald, shocking, loyal, sociable, difficult, and infinitely amusing, he inspired affection and rage with equal apparent indifference. He was like nobody else in his virtues and defects; but in a big S.C.R.[9] his failings mattered less; one forgets his occasional brutalities, and thinks of him now with real tenderness, not untouched with awe.

—*Roger Venables* *

This obituary is the work of Robert H. Dundas, the subject of Venables's book. It was published in a printed letter, corresponding to what we would call the alumni news, sent to former students at Christ Church (a college of Oxford University).

*   *   *

How would you characterize Dundas's attitudes toward Dr. Carter as a teacher? Would you call the passage sentimental? Nostalgic? Or what exactly? Would you call it admiring?

Whatever you think Dundas may think of Dr. Carter as a teacher, does he display anything in his writing that you think he might have learned from working under him?

What kind of a teacher would you call Dr. Carter? Do you think that you could learn anything from such a teacher? How do you know?

[8] A residence in London.
[9] Senior Common Room: a group made up of the head and faculty of a College.
* From *"D" Portrait of a Don* by Roger Venables, Oxford, 1967, p. 128ff. Reprinted by permission of Basil Blackwell Publisher.

*   *   *

Whatever the basis of your evaluation of the teachers you have had in the past, you have certainly had, at some time or other, a teacher you think of as good.

Choose a teacher from your experience that you would call a good teacher, one from whom you believe you learned something, and write a paper in which you show what's good about him, so far as you're concerned. What made him or makes him a good teacher? The key word here is "show." What did this teacher do, exactly? What did you do? What came of this doing? Perhaps you could write this paper as though it were a scene in a short story, a particular scene in which particular people move and speak.

Finally, look back at what you have written in your paper. Note particularly any metaphors you may have used to explain this teaching-learning process. What exactly have you defined?

Commentary

I'll begin class by collecting the papers the students have written addressing Assignment 19.

*   *   *

With this assignment (as well as with the three which follow it) we turn to some examples of teachers and teaching as a way of developing another perspective from which to see the relationship of language to the learning process.

If the diagram of the Perfect Student represents the student as object of the verb "teach" rather than free to become the subject of the verb "learn," then the Perfect Teacher can be no more than what completes the dualism, the actor on what is acted upon. I hope that this assignment will give the students an opportunity to enact their awareness that a good teacher is going to have to be talked about differently. Teaching, in other words, at least good teaching, is not simply something someone does; it is also something that is interpreted to mean good teaching by another some-one who has thereby chosen to define himself as a learner (as, for example, Hadley did; both the introductory paragraphs of the present assignment and the final paragraph of questions on the passage by Dundas are intended to open this as a way of seeing things for the students). A good teacher, therefore, I would define as someone who can enable a student to see himself as a learner; a good student is one who in seeing himself as a learner sees his teacher as a teacher. This assignment, as well as those on Agassiz, I've devised to enable us to suggest that by whatever means a teacher teaches or a learner learns, the process will invariably involve what neither the Perfect Student nor the Perfect Teacher (madmen both) is capable of: dialogue resulting in a change of language that argues a change in location that suggests a change in self. (This, by the way, is the reason I suggest the short story mode to the students.)

The Dundas passage you may or may not want to make use of in class (or have the students work with beforehand as preparation for the writing of their papers). I've included it not only because it is an example of an accomplished piece of writing which illustrates a high degree of complexity in human character, but because it describes a teacher in such a way as to define a learner, neither of which can be labeled. It is clear to me that Dundas admired Carter and for reasons analogous to those that lead me to admire the two pieces of children's writing we looked at in Assignment 9: Carter the man was Carter the teacher; Carter the teacher was Carter the man: the same manner, the same standards, the same demands were as apparent in his dealings with students and his subject as they were in his behavior as a person. But his admiration for Carter's standing for excellence in such a way as to enable excellence to stand for itself does not betray Dundas into sentimentalizing his subject. Because he never allows us to forget that Carter's "virtues and defects" were reflexes of each other, his estimate of Carter will not reduce to an easy moral equation ("Carter was cruel"; "Carter was kind"). For someone who did what he was, who had become his own style in the way that Dundas's prose suggests Carter had, things cannot be this simple. (Perhaps this, at least to judge from the way he presents Carter, is something Dundas may be said to have learned from him: making distinctions is important because the truth is important?) Carter for Dundas, as his sentences say, "was like nobody else." To go further than that I'd have to begin to quote —and then explore what I'd quoted in relation to other things I'd have to quote. It is only in these general senses that I would hope the students might see the passage as a model. (The mode we are suggesting for our students—"perhaps you could write this paper as though it were a scene in a short story"—you will notice is altogether different from Dundas's.)

I'm going to tell the students to work with the passage in light of what questions we've asked about it before they decide what kind of approach they want to take to the subject of a good teacher—mainly because I don't want to wade through a lot of silliness in this set of papers about Mr. Nice Guy and what a pal he was. Dundas's prose, I hope, will cause at least one or two students to wonder whether the ideal metaphor for the ideal teacher has to be "buddy"—or for that matter, "boss," "parent," or "entertainer." I hope, that is, that I will have at least one or two students putting some words on paper for this assignment that will create the image of a teacher and learner the only metaphor for which will be teacher and learner.

19. Wilder and Agassiz

Here is another example of a student remembering one of his former teachers:

> Agassiz handled all specimens with the greatest care, and naturally had little patience with clumsiness. . . . At one of the lectures he had handed down for inspection a very rare and costly fossil, from the coal-measures, I think; including the matrix, it had about the size and shape of the palm of the hand. He cautioned us not to drop it. When it had reached about the middle of the audience a crash was heard. The precious thing had been dropped by a new and somewhat uncouth assistant whom we will call Dr. X. He hastily gathered up the pieces and rushed out of the room. For a few seconds Agassiz stood as if himself petrified; then, without even an "Excuse me," he vanished by the same door. Presently he returned, flushed, gazing ruefully at the fragments in his hand, covered with mucilage or liquid glue. After a pause, during which those who knew him not awaited an explosive denunciation of gaucherie, Agassiz said quietly: "In natural history it is not enough to know how to study specimens; it is also necessary to know how to handle them"—and then proceeded with his lecture.

> *—Burt G. Wilder* *

One sentence from the passage above has been omitted (see ellipses). The form of it is: "The following incident illustrates both his _____ _____ [two words] and his _____ [one word]." From what you have of the passage to work with, determine what you can of what Wilder seems to think of Agassiz as a teacher, and then, just for fun, try to supply the missing three words. Why do you choose the terms you do?

Now choose three words which seem to imply something different from the words you think that Wilder may have used. How can the account be read so as to justify this second set of words as those that Wilder may have used?

What does the fact that two such readings are possible enable you to conclude about Agassiz as a teacher, about Wilder as a student, about the nature of the teaching-learning process? What did Agassiz do? What did Wilder do? What came of this doing?

* Burt G. Wilder, "Louis Agassiz, Teacher," *The Harvard Graduate Magazine,* June, 1907, pp. 47–48.

Commentary

I'll begin class by asking the students to prepare Assignment 20 for a class discussion the following period.

*　　　*　　　*

I hope that one of the things this assignment will make clear to the students about the learning process is why the Perfect Student can't learn; for there is, to the incident Wilder describes, no Reality to see (is there to any incident?). What Wilder "saw" is what he told himself he saw; what he did to make this experience an "education" was to make Agassiz into a teacher (and himself into a learner) by putting together (as Hadley did) two notions, or two languages: that of human emotion (anger, sorrow, whatever) with the idea of Agassiz as an instructor. Hence the episode "illustrates" Agassiz's "kindly spirit and his self-restraint"—because that is what Wilder made it into by naming it as he does.

The fun of this assignment will lie in our defining ourselves against the students' definitions of the Wilder passage as a learning experience. I'm not interested so much in whether the students guess that the account is laudatory (possibly some of them will work on the assumption that an article with the title of Wilder's would not have appeared in *The Harvard Graduate Magazine* unless it *were* laudatory; maybe some will have already read Assignment 20), but I am interested in how many will be able to see that from another point of view the incident could just as easily be said to illustrate Agassiz's caustic wit or cold-heartedness or calculated cruelty. (I think I will mimeograph as my first "paper" a number of different choices that I'll either take from what the students write or make up in order to demonstrate how virtually any kind of pairing could be made to work in Wilder's context. I plan also, before class actually starts, to choose a student whose spirit I think I know and speak sharply, perhaps even semi-rudely, to him over what could be called a "violation" of the educational process. He'll be talking to someone when I'm ready to begin class, for example, or laughing, or he won't have brought his book, or he will have been ten seconds late—anything that I can behave with in such a way as to enable us to talk later in the period about whether my behavior was "bad-tempered" or "for the students' own good" or, as the case will be, "contrived to make a point." My point will be, of course, that no one is going to be able to tell what the case really was, no matter what I claim it was.)

I am particularly interested in what the students will do with the last paragraph of questions in the assignment. I have in mind no master realization, but I will be looking for the students to do something with the notion of the teaching-learning process as involving both choice and opportunity. (Isn't there a way in which Wilder may be said to have "learned" a great deal more than that Agassiz had a kindly spirit and could be self-restrained?) It would make my day, of course, to have someone extend this to consider the importance that faith and chance seem to play in the process as well—that which so often makes the core of so much education so much more mysterious than I can afford to behave as though I knew.

20. Shaler and Agassiz

Here is another estimate of Louis Agassiz as a teacher. Again, the writer is one of his former students, N. S. Shaler, who studied zoology under Agassiz as an undergraduate at Harvard and later became a Professor of Geology at the same University. The passage is taken from *The Autobiography of Nathaniel Southgate Shaler.*

When I sat me down before my tin pan, Agassiz brought me a small fish, placing it before me with the rather stern requirement that I should study it, but should on no account talk to any one concerning it, nor read anything relating to fishes, until I had his permission so to do. To my inquiry, "What shall I do?" he said in effect: "Find out what you can without damaging the specimen; when I think that you have done the work I will question you." In the course of an hour I thought I had compassed that fish; it was rather an unsavory object, giving forth the stench of old alcohol, then loathsome to me, though in time I came to like it. Many of the scales were loosened so that they fell off. It appeared to me to be a case for a summary report, which I was anxious to make and get on to the next stage of the business. But Agassiz, though always within call, concerned himself no further with me that day, nor the next, nor for a week. At first, this neglect was distressing; but I saw that it was a game, for he was, as I discerned rather than saw, covertly watching me. So I set my wits to work upon the thing, and in the course of a hundred hours or so thought I had done much—a hundred times as much as seemed possible at the start. I got interested in finding out how the scales went in series, their shape, the form and placement of the teeth, etc. Finally, I felt full of the subject, and probably expressed it in my bearing; as for words about it then, there were none from my master except his cheery "Good morning." At length, on the seventh day, came the question, "Well?" and my disgorge of learning to him as he sat on the edge of my table puffing his cigar. At the end of the hour's telling, he swung off and away, saying: "That is not right." Here I began to think that, after all, perhaps the rules for scanning Latin verse were not the worst infliction in the world. Moreover, it was clear that he was playing a game with me to find if I were capable of doing hard, continuous work without the support of a teacher, and this stimulated me to labor. I went at the task anew, discarded my first notes, and in another week of ten hours a day labor I had results which astonished myself and satisfied him. Still there was no trace of praise in words or manner. He signified that it would do by placing before me about a half a peck of bones, telling me to see what I could make of them, with no further directions to guide me. I soon found that they were the skeletons of half a dozen fishes of different species; the jaws told me so much at a first inspection. The task evidently was to fit the separate bones together in their proper order. Two months or more went to this task with no other help than an occasional looking over my grouping with the stereotyped remark: "That is not right." Finally, the task was done, and I was again set upon alcoholic specimens—this time a remarkable lot of specimens representing, perhaps, twenty species of the side-swimmers or Pleuronectidae.

I shall never forget the sense of power in dealing with things which I felt in beginning the more extended work on a group of animals. I had learned the art of comparing objects, which is the basis of the naturalist's work. At this stage I was allowed to read, and to discuss my work with others about me. I did both eagerly, and acquired a considerable knowledge of the literature of ichthyology, becoming especially interested in the system of classification, then most imperfect. I tried to follow Agassiz's scheme of division into the order of ctenoids and ganoids, with the result that I found one of my species of side-swimmers had cycloid scales on one side and ctenoid on the other. This not only shocked my sense of the value of classification in a way that permitted of no full recovery of my original respect for the process, but for a time shook my confidence in my master's knowledge. At the same time I had a malicious pleasure in exhibiting my "find" to him expecting to repay in part the humiliation which he had evidently tried to inflict on my conceit. To my question as to how the nondescript should be classified he said: "My boy, there are now two of us who know that."

At the time of the events narrated by Shaler (1859–1860) there were no written examinations on any subjects to be taken by candidates for the Scientific School (as the College of Science at Harvard was then called). Admission to a course of study was by permission of the professors in charge of the several departments who questioned candidates orally in order to determine their fitness to proceed for a degree. The students who were accepted paid their fees directly to their teachers who depended on such additions to their salaries in order to live. (In 1859, for example, Agassiz was paid only $2,500 a year in salary by the University, a sum that Shaler himself calls "meager.") "Few or none," Shaler remarks, "who had any semblance of an education were denied admission to Agassiz's laboratory." But a number of those granted admission stayed there a good deal longer than the four years required for a degree. For Agassiz refused to recommend the graduation of "some who had been with him for many years, and had succeeded in their special work, giving as reason for his denial that they were 'too ignorant.' " Shaler recalls that the preliminary examination Agassiz gave him "was directed first to find that I knew enough Latin and Greek to make use of those languages." Then came a test in German and French. He seemed not at all interested, Shaler states, "to find what I knew about fossils, rocks, animals and plants"—at which the student was, of course, "offended." On the day that Shaler sat him down before that tin pan, Agassiz's laboratory consisted of "one room about thirty feet long and fifteen feet wide" the whole of which was invariably "packed" with students. The rest of the "two story building" was given over to storerooms in which Agassiz's "collections were crammed." In this, his second meeting with Agassiz, Shaler was simply assigned a place at "a small pine table." The tin pan before him he remembers distinctly as being very rusty.

What did Shaler learn from Agassiz so far as you are concerned? Locate as specifically as you can some instances of this learning. What sentences and terms do you go to? What do you say that this learning consists of?

Is what Shaler seems to think he learned from Agassiz the same thing that Agassiz taught him? Is what he seems to think he learned the same thing as what he did learn? What does Shaler seem to think of Agassiz as a teacher?

Where do you find yourself with Agassiz as a teacher, with the whole process of teaching and learning as it was conducted in 1859–60 or thereabouts? Can you imagine electing to study under such a man in such a system? How would you respond to a teacher who made it very clear to you that you would need his "permission" to read about a subject, or who told you after you had worked for seven days on something simply that what you had done wasn't "right"? What would you think of a physics teacher who used your ability to write a sentence in English as a gauge for your fitness to study physics? How would you respond to a teacher with "no trace of praise in words or manner"? Or would it depend? On what? Are you accustomed to seeing teachers as out to inflict humiliation on your conceit? Is that a right you are accustomed to grant them? Or do you have another way of understanding the process of teaching and learning?

And what about those working conditions, the rusty equipment, everybody crammed into one room of a two story house the rest of which was made into storerooms for Agassiz's collections? Would you resent a comparable situation in your own education? To judge from what Shaler says above, how do you imagine he saw the conditions under which he worked? (Just by the way, the omitted sentence from the passage by Wilder given you on the last assignment reads as follows: "The following incident illustrates both his kindly spirit and his self-restraint.") When you compare yourself as a student with Shaler what similarities do you find? Any differences?

*　　*　　*

N.B. When you come to class know who Louis Agassiz was and, again, be able to supply the printed source or sources for your information.

Commentary

I'll begin class with a five-minute quiz on Agassiz. I'll then ask the students to prepare Assignment 21 for a class discussion the next period and tell them also to write a paper addressing Assignment 22 to be turned in the same period.

*　　*　　*

In a way, the two assignments on Agassiz are the heart of the course, though for students they will probably not be that until later—perhaps long after the course is over. When I say "the heart of the course" I mean first of all that our procedure in the course, all these bones we have been laying out for students to make some sort of order of, is an obvious analogue of Agassiz's methodology—even though our "that is not right" can never be what Agassiz's was, can have reference only to our private definitions of correctness, intelligence, liveliness of imagination, and so on. Second, I mean that however you may have been looking at our nominal subject of teaching and learning in relationship to the subject of language, the two assignments on Agassiz should make clear the dependence of one on the other.

My way of taking up this dependence with my students is going to be to use the two assignments on Agassiz as a way of suggesting that teaching and learning mean only what they are made to mean—by teachers as well as by students. The process is made meaningful through the learner's development of a language which enables him to rename, reinterpret, re-create his experience in such a way as to cause him to become more than he was. (Generally, this "development of a language" would seem to involve a putting together of one way of naming with another in order to come up with a third way of naming; that is, with a way of seeing made up of various other ways of seeing that are fused into a new vision. Hence Shaler at first sees the fish as just "a case for a summary report." Agassiz's swinging off and away with his "That is not right" implies another way of seeing the fish. It is Shaler's putting together of these two ways of seeing which eventuates in another kind of report, in those "results" which astonish him and satisfy Agassiz, that could be called a third way of seeing. This notion of the putting together of languages to develop a new language we return to in Assignments 22 and 23.) From this point of view, I would say that Malcolm X, Franklin, Hadley, and Shaler were all successful learners. Each, in his own way, in changing how he named what he was looking at, changed what he saw. Each in changing what he saw changed who he was.

A good teacher, then, makes it possible for students to be students, to be learners. I would say that Agassiz was a good teacher because he put his students into a position to choose whether they were going to see themselves as learners by choosing to see him as a teacher or not. He did more than give his students (or at least Shaler) a language for their experience with natural history; he gave them what (at least for some) compelled them to develop a language for that experience themselves (which is the significance of Shaler's saying: "I had learned the art of comparing objects"—a process, notice, not a thing; and a process he says he learned rather than was taught); he gave them a vocabulary for which they had to become the syntax. I would say, then, that in offering a style as the invitation to develop a style, Agassiz offered Shaler an opportunity to become Shaler—an effect of the teaching-learning process that both men experienced without necessarily being conscious of it in those terms. This is part of what I mean by claiming that education involves a mystery.

I include the background material I do for the Shaler passage primarily to suggest that Shaler, like Wilder, made a choice in how he was going to see Agassiz and his methods, and that by someone else the experience that Shaler found so richly educational might have been seen as demeaning or senseless. It would be possible for someone to see Agassiz as a tyrant (remembering those students he wouldn't recommend for a degree), or as selfish (in his keeping the larger part of that two story building for his own use), or as bitterly mercenary. Those jammed and smelly rooms, the rusty equipment: would not these have "turned off" (the metaphor is appropriate) our Perfect Student? Would he have been able to see those working conditions in the way that Shaler's behavior suggests he might have: as the evidence of how much a dedicated man was willing to sacrifice for his commitment to a discipline? Would the Perfect Student have been willing to allow for the possibility that Agassiz's treatment of students (like Carter's) might have emerged from caring, a concern— for them as well as for a subject? Would he have seen that examination in Latin and Greek, French and German, as perhaps Agassiz's way of finding out what kind of sustained rote learning he was capable of, or as Agassiz's way of acquainting him with what it meant to be educated? We know, of course, where the Perfect Student would have been with Agassiz, because we know where he is on the subject of learning. What I'd like the latter part of this assignment to offer students, however, is a way of seeing what there might be for them in being other, more, better than the Perfect Student is.

21. Teaching and Learning: A Situation

Here is a sketch that involves the subject of learning:

"Man, I remember something when I was little, a boy," somebody named Lee says. He is hunched forward, his elbows on the table, a tumbler of wine between his hands. "About a dog. Little miserable dog of mine."

"Yeah, man, go on," Mike says, his eyes lighting up.

"I get up real early to do my paper route. Los Angeles *Examiner*," Lee says. "Streets always empty, just a few milk trucks and bakery trucks and other kids like me. My dog goes along, see? Every day he trots along with me. Little mongrel dog."

"Yeah, yeah, go on, man," Mike says, impatient for the story, sure that it has meaning.

"There we are in all those big empty streets. Just me and the dog. Sun coming up, papers falling on the porches, me dreaming and walking and the dog trotting," Lee says. "Then far away, about as big as a black mosquito, I see this hopped-up Model A. Wonderful pipes on it, blatting so sweet I could hear them for six blocks. I stand there on the curb, listening to that sweet sound and watching that car come weaving down that empty street. And the dog stands in the gutter, watching too. That Model A gets bigger and I can see the chrome pipes on the side, the twin Strombergs sucking air, just eating up the asphalt."

He pauses and Mike leans forward and says urgently, "Now man, come on, go. I wanna hear this."

"This Model A is a roadster and there is a Mexican driving and his girl with him," Lee says slowly, stalking the climax. "It weaves across the street, and me and the dog stare at it. And it comes for us in a big slow curve and hit that dog. His back broke in mid-air and he was dead when he hit the street again. Like a big man cracking a seed in his teeth . . . same sound, I mean. And the girl stares back at me and laughs. And I laugh. You see why, man?"

The two of them sit quietly, looking down at the wine and listening to the jazz. Mike glances once at Lee and then back at his glass. He has learned something secret and private about Lee, and that is good enough. After a while they sit back, smiling, and listen to the jazz.

—Eugene Burdick *

* Eugene Burdick, "The Innocent Nihilists Adrift in Squaresville," *The Reporter*, April 1958, p. 33. Reprinted by permission of Curtis Brown, Ltd. Copyright © 1958 by Eugene Burdick.

Burdick shapes his account in such a way as to cast Lee in the conventional role of teacher, Mike in the conventional role of student. What sort of teacher does Burdick seem to think that Lee is? What sort of student does he seem to think Mike is? To judge from your understanding of what Burdick has written, what does he seem to think is taught on this occasion? What is learned?

In a sense, Burdick the writer is also a teacher. We his readers are students. In presenting the relationship between Lee and Mike as he does here, what does Burdick teach about teaching and learning? What meaning do you as a reader-student make of Burdick's teaching?

Commentary

I'll begin class by collecting the papers the students have written addressing Assignment 22.

*   *   *

"But doesn't this (meaning our discussions on Agassiz particularly, though the reference may well extend beyond the last two assignments) mean that a teacher can do just anything that he wants to do and that it's up to the student to make some sense of the doing? Doesn't it mean also that any sense made by any student of what a teacher does is just as good as any other?"

Whether the students have openly articulated such questions for themselves or not, I think that this is an appropriate point in our sequence to raise them. The Answer, obviously, to the two questions is "no," but the assignment, you will notice, is concerned with enabling the student to make that Answer mean something, with enabling each student to develop an explanation for the why of it (in terms of the sketch by Burdick) that will turn the Answer into his answer, into an answer for him.

I think that what Burdick teaches in his sketch is that teaching and learning have to do more than look like teaching and learning in order to amount to anything. Or one could say that he teaches that the illusion of communication passes most easily for the real thing among people who don't know very much about the relationship of teaching and learning to language. Or, it is easier to think you are teaching or learning than to do it. There are a lot of ways to talk about Burdick's sketch in relation to both our real and our nominal subjects, and even more ways to talk about the application of it to one's experience with the teaching-learning process. These will be the matters that I want my class to conclude with. I would be surprised if when we get there the students aren't able to come up with possibilities for seeing Burdick's sketch that I haven't been able to imagine.

I want first, however, to take up the question of the way Lee and Mike are presented as teacher and student, and I intend to do this by following a procedure similar to that I used with Wilder's account of Agassiz in Assignment 19. I'll start out by focusing the students on what for me is the key moment in the sketch: "And I laugh. You see why, man?" Why did Lee laugh, I'll ask, and what does he mean by asking Mike whether he sees why he did? It is impossible to tell in either case so far as I'm concerned. Lee could mean: I laughed to show I wasn't defeated, or I laughed to show I was, or I laughed because they thought the dog was important to me when I knew he wasn't, or I laughed to keep from crying —the possibilities are numerous. Similarly, does Lee ask Mike the question he does to ask for help in working something out, or because he wants to test Mike's loyalty, or because he wants to see whether Mike can catch onto a joke, or to prove to himself that Mike is a fool? There is simply no way of knowing, and reference to the context of the moment (Why did the man hit the dog? What did Lee really think of the dog? Why did the girl laugh?) only compounds the dilemma. To be sure, there was no way of Wilder's knowing what Agassiz might have thought and felt and meant either, but the difference is that whereas Agassiz provided his students with a way of seeing "what happened" as a way of knowing about both a subject and their relationship to it (whatever his motives for doing so), Lee's behavior and language totally eliminate the possibility of his "student's" developing a way of knowing anything at all about the subject here—him. Since the subject is ostensibly that of self-revelation, Lee's motives are important, and yet a reader can't tell any better than Mike can whether Lee is (and was) being super-crafty, irresponsible, or just plain stupid in behaving as he does (and did).

The form of a teaching-learning situation in this instance becomes an assurance that nothing will have been taught or learned. What seems communicated between Lee and Mike is that there will be no communication. For Mike is as much of a mock student as Lee is a mock teacher, and not, as with Lee, because we do not know why he behaves as he does. Mike is a mock-student, Burdick suggests (in saying that he is "impatient for the story, sure that it has meaning" and later: "He has learned something secret and private about Lee, and that is good enough"), because he decides (in the moment of his glancing "once at Lee") to give up his identity as a student (the way, in this case, to his identity as a person) in order to become the Perfect Student (settling for the lowest common denominator of "Reality as it really is") without being in any way aware that that is what he has done. When teaching is the giving of sensation only, and learning no more than getting a sensation, any sensation—then of course it doesn't matter what the teacher and the learner do.

22. *A Flash of Insight*

Here is an account of an act of learning:

> . . . Edison created the phonograph in a single day in 1877. Years before . . . a phenomenon occurred while he was experimenting upon the idea of sending a telegraph signal from a whirling disc upon which a stylus pricked electromagnetic embossed telegraphic dots and dashes, creating a musical hum when the disc whirled at high speed. In 1877 he developed a funnel-like toy. When he talked through the funnel, the vibrations caused by his voice worked a pawl which turned a ratchet wheel connected by a pulley with a paper figure of a man operating a paper saw on a paper log. Edison noted that at times the man moved rhythmically, at times jerkily, depending upon the words shouted at the horn and the pitch of his voice. Out of the setting of the musical hum, noted years previously, and the industrious paper man sawing his paper log came the *flash of insight* which produced a phonograph in thirty hours.
>
> —*Austin L. Porterfield* *

At one time or another you have certainly had what is referred to above as a "flash of insight." When you look back over your experience, you can isolate a moment of illumination, of things coming together so that as it turned out, you had an idea, saw a solution, knew what to do.

See if you can recapture such a moment and put it on paper. The resulting "new idea" may not really be a very new idea at all. Yet it was good enough for you at the moment and you took some satisfaction in it.

On the basis of what you have written, what would you say is involved in a "flash of insight"? What exactly got put together with what? What was the result of this putting together?

Commentary

I'll begin by asking the students to prepare Assignment 23 for a class discussion next time. I'll also have them write a paper addressing Assignment 24 to be turned in the same period.

* * *

* From *Creative Factors in Scientific Research* by Austin L. Porterfield, Duke University Press, 1941, p. 95. Reprinted by permission of Duke University Press.

"A flash of insight" like the phrase "change of mind" I see as a metaphoric designation of a moment when one language or one way of seeing gives way to another. But since both a flash of insight and a change of mind can be seen as acts of learning, another way of putting this, as I have already suggested, is to say that one language would seem to combine with another language in order to form a third language. For though sometimes the change involved can feel very dramatic indeed ("Suddenly I realized I had never loved her at all"), at other times there seems less to be a replacement of one way of looking at things by another than a complication of a way of seeing that comes with, say, a different or fuller definition of terms (Wordsworth's "huge peak" in the passage from *The Prelude* used in Assignment 4, for example, never stops being a peak for all the poet's anthropomorphizing of it—one of the reasons the passage works so well). But I do not know of a change in mind or of a flash of insight that does not depend upon a change in language of some sort, and this is what I would like to use this assignment and the students' papers addressed to it to demonstrate.

Any paper in which anyone tries to describe a moment when things came together to produce a flash of insight, any paper written with any kind of fidelity to the experience being talked about, I think will demonstrate that a change in language (a broadening, a widening, a redefinition of terms) necessarily precedes the getting of an idea, the seeing of a solution, knowing what to do. In the papers written by those students who decide to be other than Themewriters for this assignment, we will find something analagous to what can be traced out in Porterfield's passage about Edison. The basis for Edison's insight would seem to be the sharing of a single term by two different contexts (or language systems), the term "sound." In one context "sound" is only "a musical hum" produced by "a whirling disk." In the second context, "sound" is "vibrations" that vary with what words are spoken and with the pitch of the voice. "Phonograph" (or some conceptual equivalent of the term) is a combining of these two senses of the term "sound," the putting together of "vibrations" with "musical hum" produced by "a whirling disk" in such a way as to eventuate in a concept of sound impulses recorded on a disk which may be whirled to reproduce the sound of music. Similarly, Wordsworth's "huge peak" makes capital of our use of "huge" to describe effects and people as well as things, and of the double sense of the word "head" in the conclusion of the sentence:

> . . . a huge peak, black and huge,
> As if with voluntary power instinct,
> Upreared its head.

What comes together in Wordsworth's lines is the notion of the mountain peak as a mountain peak with the notion of it as animate; the terminology of one language system or context (landscape) overlaps with or opens into another (people) by means of a term (or series of them) that both systems share but define differently. It is this merging that eventuates in the creation of a third system: Wordsworth's notion of an animated universe. It is in the combining of these two (or more) contexts to produce a third that the flash of insight is to be located. I want to spend the class period finding that momentary point of contact, that moment with language, in students' papers. For to see a use of language as the prerequisite for an idea is but another way of suggesting why it is important to use language responsibly.

23. Writing as Learning

This assignment gives you the opportunity to define the development of a piece of writing and to conclude what you can about the meaning of the process.

Like you, the writer of the versions of the paper reproduced here was a student in a composition course. The first version of the paper was required. That is, it was a paper written to address a specific writing assignment. The second and third versions the writer did on her own. The assignment read as follows:

> We often say in this course that a writer ought to write about what he knows. Let us assume for the sake of this paper that one thing all of us know is this school and its surroundings. We are speaking now of the school in terms of its physical thereness, its location and arrangement as a place.
>
> Describe some part of Drexel University as you see it. The emphasis here is on both the word "see" and the word "you." That is, take care that you don't swallow up the scene with metaphor, but try to make what you see an image of what *you* see (not of what just anybody could see). Perhaps you would find it most fruitful to work with something about which you have some ambiguity of attitude, about which you feel more than one way. Try also to avoid obvious cop-outs: "The cafeteria at lunchtime is certainly a scene of varied activity," etc.

The following pages show the three versions of the paper.

Here is the first version of the paper as marked by the teacher:

~~The beauty of the Asbury church~~ comes from its con-
~~trasts. From its appearance on~~ the outside, I would not
~~suspect that it had any~~ connection with Drexel--in other
The Asbury Church is
words, ~~it's~~ not made of orange brick. It is a big, solid-
looking, old building. ~~This~~ oldness ~~is one of the quali-~~
~~ties that appeals to me. In comparison with the rest of~~
~~the University area, the uniform, "modern" architecture,~~
~~Asbury has character and stability.~~

Let a reader say this.

→ *Now go on so that a reader can say "Its beauty is its contrast. It's unlike the rest of Drexel," etc.*

Inside the building in the sanctuary is the same
atmosphere. It is a huge room, with a ceiling two stories
up, lined with stained glass windows, (the picture of an)
old-fashioned church.

This is the tip-off that you're working with clichés.

And yet what goes on inside is anything but old-
fashioned. The service is <u>creative</u> and bears almost no
resemblance to a <u>normal</u>, <u>conventional</u> service. The min-
isters are <u>young</u> and <u>interested in the Universities</u> and
the community. There are projects aimed at actively attacking some of the <u>problems in Philadelphia</u>.

Can't you hear how these are close-out terms -generalizations that bury what you see?

Possibly my reaction is a form of rebellion, although
one I won't admit to. The church I attended before coming
to Philadelphia is a typical suburban church--a small
the building is?
redwood building that is <u>fairly well landscaped,</u> and has
a standard service. While Asbury is old-fashioned and
slightly crumbling, it is also very now.

Again--do the scene so that the scene says this.

With control the metaphor might work.

Here is the second version as marked:

Now, you have a subjec. It's more than a, church you're talking about.

The Asbury Church is not made of orange brick. It is an old stone building.

These details don't seem pointed enough.

There are rows and rows of long pews, with designs carved in the wood. Probably 400 people could attend, although 40 is a crowd. The stained glass windows are big; they fill the walls. Very bright colors echo on the floor.

Underneath so much stillness is a lot of activity that can't be seen. Only occasionally do the sounds of the people staying in the weekend shelter downstairs make their way up here into the sanctuary. Some of those people are wearing awfully old, unmatched clothes, and

And? Can you extend the ambiguity here or fill it out?

they don't look clean and happy and thankful *as* like you're supposed to in a church.

The organ fills a large corner, as if the pipes are growing there. They look too big, almost. The ceiling is so far away, it is *you...* almost forgotten. It encloses the room--the area, but only in that it shuts out the outside; it adds to the feeling of space.

¶ ? There are always enormous areas that are motionless.

There's not enough precision in the finish here for me. Maybe you need some suggestion of your having re-seen the church.

Here is the third version:

Unlike the rest of Drexel, the Asbury Church is not
made of orange brick. It is an old, beautifully fitted
stone building.

There are rows and rows of long pews, all of them
with designs carved deep in the black wood. Probably
400 people could attend a service, although most Sundays
40 is a crowd. The stained glass windows seem to have
swallowed the walls. The sun throws its bright colors
into pleasant patterns on the floor. Most of the time,
even on Sundays, it is very, very still.

Underneath the stillness is a lot of activity that
can't be seen. But only occasionally do the sounds of
the people staying in the weekend shelter downstairs
make their way up here into the sanctuary. Most of the
people down there wear old, unmatched clothes. They don't
look clean and happy and thankful the way you're supposed
to look in a church. A lot of them are activists of one
sort or another. They share their meals.

The organ fills a large corner looking as if its
pipes are growing there. They look too big, almost.
The ceiling is so far away you almost forget about it.
It encloses things but only in that it shuts out the
outside; inside it adds to the feeling of space. There
are always enormous areas of motionlessness. Sometimes
the quiet seems almost dead still.

One way of preparing yourself to address the following questions might be to imagine how you would mark the third version of this paper if you were the teacher of this student in this course. (We are speaking of more here than the assigning of a grade.) Suppose that in addition to your marginalia, you felt compelled to write a final comment on the paper. What would it be? What would you expect the student to understand by it?

How would you describe what it is that seems to happen from version to version of this paper? From what to what does the paper move, exactly? How would you evaluate this movement? Does the student have anything at the end of the process that she didn't have at the beginning of it? How about the teacher?

What part did the teacher play in the process? What did he do?

What part did the student play in the process? What did *she* do?

On the basis of what you have said so far, define "teacher" in the development of this piece of writing. Then define "student."

Commentary

I'll begin class by collecting the papers addressed to Assignment 24.

*　　*　　*

There are a lot of ways this assignment can be brought into the context of what we have been considering from the beginning. It is obvious, for example, that one way in which the movement of the versions of the paper can be described is to say that the writer stops Themewriting and begins writing. Important also are the ways in which the writer here has seen her role as a student (and how the teacher behaves as a teacher); for it is not so simple as saying that the teacher says "do this" and the student then does it. The teacher can be seen providing terms from which a language must be made; the student, in her writing, may be seen making of these terms a language for herself—sometimes successfully (so far as I am concerned), sometimes not so successfully. Finally, the movement of the three versions of this paper enacts the putting together of one language (the original paper) with another (the teacher's comments) in order to develop a third (the last two versions of the paper). But for me, the key question of this assignment is going to be "From what to what does this paper move exactly?" and "Has the student got anything at the end of the process that she didn't have at the beginning of it?" I intend to address these questions in class by doing what I can to make the period a way of distinguishing bad literature from literature, non-art from art, in terms of what this distinction involves for the artist.

I don't suppose that at this point we will have much trouble with the students' being able to identify the movement of the three versions of the paper as a movement from the general to the specific, the abstract to the concrete, the simple-minded to the complex (though I expect we'll all be busy for most of the class getting our students to earn these generalizations, to specify, for example, what has happened to the flaccid "it is very now" by the time it shows up in version III in the form of that marvelously ambiguous paragraph on the "activists"; or to notice the way in which "stillness" and "quiet" in the later versions become metaphorically suggestive of stasis and deadness; and so on). But what the students may not be so quick to understand is the way in which this process enacts not just the discovery of a voice of one's own, but the meaning of having one, the value of art (of writing) for the artist (for the writer). For the marvel of the three versions of that paper to me is the way in which they dramatize not what Good Writing is (what is it?), but what there can be in the writing process for anyone who chooses to involve himself with it. Anyone. Not just someone with a Talent for Expression or a Flair for Words. (The student who did that paper is not what I would call a gifted writer. Some details in even the third version are not rendered with very much precision ["beautifully fitted stone building"]. Undoubtedly, none of us would have any trouble developing other ways of talking about how even the final version has flaws.)

What I will be trying to make the class on this assignment say to students, therefore, is not just: "Look what this writer came from" or "Look at how much this writer did with what she had to work with in the way of native ability." I will want the class also to be a way of suggesting what the writer might have learned about her relationship to her religious faith through her doing what she did as a student in a composition course. The real value of that paper lies in the self-clarification that the writing of it seems to have brought the writer through her facing as a dilemma what at first she doesn't recognize as even a conflict, let alone a conflict of any importance to her. The "improvement" in the paper from this point of view is really a matter of self-discovery, the development of a nobody into someone, the movement from blindness to sight to insight. In coming to look at an "it" in such a way as to bring herself into touch with a "she," with a self that it is hard to imagine has not grown through that acknowledgment, this writer, as a writer for herself, becomes her most important reader. To be sure, the writer does not resolve the conflict between her past and her present, but perhaps in refusing to oversimplify herself by oversimplifying the terms of it, an honesty which suggests a readiness to live out the implications of that conflict—perhaps in this there is resolution of another, of a higher sort.

No teacher can "teach" the growth of self-awareness implicit in the movement of the three versions of that paper; this writer came to that awareness by and for herself. On the other hand, she did not come to what she came to alone; and if her teacher did not create her self-awareness, what he said and did were part of what made her movement toward it possible. It's the sort of thing, at least occasionally, that all of us as teachers can look to have a share in.

24. Why Doesn't Education Work Better?

Even with the best will in the world, and no matter how experienced or skilled they may be, teachers do not always teach. Nor do students, even when they are intelligent, highly-motivated, well-prepared, etc., always learn.

What's the trouble here? Why doesn't an educational institution work better than it does? Why doesn't education work better than it does—even when everyone wants it to?

Address these questions by examining your relation to your own learning at the educational institution you are attending. What are the fundamental difficulties you encounter even when you want to learn, even when you make up your mind to work at it? What would you say are the greatest barriers to your learning inside an educational institution?

Can you think of any alternatives to the system of formal education as you know it? Another system? The abolition of institutionalized education altogether?

Commentary

I'll begin by asking the class to prepare Assignment 25 for discussion for the next period.

* * *

In this assignment we again shift the perspective from which we have been seeing our subjects. Asking the students as we do here to confront the question of what seem to them the biggest barriers to education under even optimum circumstances is a first step in an attempt to involve us with some of the paradoxes of the educational process and therefore with the ambiguity of our attitudes toward it. For though in this assignment we are concerned only with why the process of education as a process (as that which no one would want to subvert, question, resist, or openly interfere with particularly) should work no better than it does, our final question for the students ("Can you think of any alternatives to the system of formal education as you know it?") carries us to the edge of other questions which Assignments 25 through 29 should enable the students to isolate and address. All of these questions have to do in one way or another with what could be called the risk of education (the risk of language-using) and with what may be said to make the risk worth taking.

What we are asking the students to do in this paper is to take a position rather than to come up with an answer, for the problem of the assignment is to find terms from one's own educational experience to show what it means to say that it isn't easy to make someone else's language a language for one's self, or to have to create a syntax in order to make sense of a vocabulary—even when one is quite clear that that is what has to be done, even when one might want to. He with his languages is who he is; I with mine am I. What I'll be looking for in the students' papers, then, are sentences that seem born of a realization that an intelligent consideration of the problem here cannot blame what it is conventional to blame for the failure or the difficulty of education and get very far (though even with our attempts to forestall it, I'm sure that along with the familiar example of the teacher who "knows his field but can't put the material across," we'll have students talking about how awful procrastination is or admitting that they've always had trouble concentrating). I'll be looking also for some indication that the ritualistic invocation of phrases like "failure of communication" won't get a writer very far either. In other words, I'll be ready to praise any writer who makes an attempt on this paper to see the barriers to education as other than a matter of bad faith or bad character and as more than a matter of clichés—the *almost right* that in being almost right in the way that it is is wronger than wrong.

In a very real sense what seems to get in the way of education, even when everyone claims to want it to work, *is* character, not "bad character," but human character; and "failure of communication" is what would seem to be the result of its workings. But to say this in just that way is to see very little of what is involved in the saying; it is to see a matter of phenomenology as a question of morals—"if only we all *tried* harder." There is this, of course, but I don't know whether that stance is going to address, say, my sense of aloneness, my feelings of helplessness as a teacher sometimes, in the face of a given language pattern of my students ("never trust a Black"; "all government is corrupt"), a pattern I know to be interlocked with other language patterns, the whole of which I know also to be a matter of who they are, how they get along and have gotten along in the world. It isn't just *one* language pattern that I have to deal with; you can't know or learn or teach just one thing that way. But how, then, do I deal with what makes the pattern a pattern?

I remember my attempts as a student to "understand" the anthropological ideas of Margaret Mead; my problem as I see it now was really a matter of what I was trying to understand her ideas with, of who I was then, of the assumptions I had that I didn't know I had that kept me even from seeing an idea as the idea it was when I thought that I *did* see it. My problem, in other words, was not just the conventional problem of not "understanding" what I was reading; it was also a matter of not realizing that even what I thought I understood I did not in fact understand at all. "In fact" and "As I see it now." For the question immediately arises of what I will read Margaret Mead with ten years from now. And does this mean that I should not have read Margaret Mead when I first did? That I should not read her ever?

Clearly, this is more than a moral matter. Perhaps the question is not one of why education doesn't work better, but why it works at all. Perhaps the trouble lies not with education but with our confusion of what education can do with what it cannot do if it is to remain education, a system in which students are students and not disciples or sheep, in which teachers are teachers and not prophets. If we had a system of education in which education worked better, in which teachers gave students the languages they were to learn instead of what the students were expected to make their own languages from, a system in which teachers "taught" students to "apply" their rote learning instead of demanding that they find ways of applying it for themselves—then would it be *education* we were talking about? This is why the question of alternatives to formal education has always seemed to me a more complex matter than the proponents of it make out. Certainly there are alternative systems of formal education, but whether there is an alternative to a system I am not so sure. The classroom in the open air would seem either to be another system, or something other than education. From this point of view, perhaps the greatest barrier to learning inside a system of formal education is precisely what formal education was set up as a system to deal with. Perhaps education is most education when it exists for no reason other than to make it possible for someone to do what it as a system cannot.

25. Lewis Padgett

The following science fiction story may be read as a statement about the relationship of teaching and learning as processes of language.

Mimsy Were the Borogoves

by Lewis Padgett *

There's no use trying to describe either Unthahorsten or his surroundings, because, for one thing, a good many million years had passed since 1942 Anno Domini, and, for another, Unthahorsten wasn't on Earth, technically speaking. He was doing the equivalent of standing in the equivalent of a laboratory. He was preparing to test his time machine.

Having turned on the power, Unthahorsten suddenly realized that the Box was empty. Which wouldn't do at all. The device needed a control, a three-dimensional solid which would react to the conditions of another age. Otherwise Unthahorsten couldn't tell, on the machine's return, where and when it had been. Whereas a solid in the Box would automatically be subject to the entropy and cosmic ray bombardment of the other era, and Unthahorsten could measure the changes, both qualitative and quantitative, when the machine returned. The Calculators could then get to work and, presently, tell Unthahorsten that the Box had briefly visited 1,000,000 A.D., 1,000 A.D., or 1 A.D., as the case might be.

Not that it mattered, except to Unthahorsten. But he was childish in many respects.

There was little time to waste. The Box was beginning to glow and shiver. Unthahorsten stared around wildly, fled into the next glossatch, and groped in a storage bin there. He came up with an armful of peculiar-looking stuff. Uh-huh. Some of the discarded toys of his son Snowen, which the boy had brought with him when he had passed over from Earth, after mastering the necessary technique. Well, Snowen needed this junk no longer. He was conditioned, and had put away childish things. Besides, though Unthahorsten's wife kept the toys for sentimental reasons, the experiment was more important.

* First published in 1943 ("Lewis Padgett" was a pseudonym employed by Henry Kuttner and his wife, C. L. Moore). Copyright © 1954 by Lewis Padgett. Reprinted by permission of Harold Matson Co., Inc.

Unthahorsten left the glossatch and dumped the assortment into the Box, slamming the cover shut just before the warning signal flashed. The Box went away. The manner of its departure hurt Unthahorsten's eyes.

He waited.

And he waited.

Eventually he gave up and built another time machine, with identical results. Snowen hadn't been annoyed by the loss of his old toys, nor had Snowen's mother, so Unthahorsten cleaned out the bin and dumped the remainder of his son's childhood relics in the second time machine's Box.

According to his calculations, this one should have appeared on Earth, in the latter part of the nineteenth century, A.D. If that actually occurred, the device remained there.

Disgusted, Unthahorsten decided to make no more time machines. But the mischief had been done. There were two of them, and the first—

Scott Paradine found it while he was playing hooky from the Glendale Grammar School. There was a geography test that day, and Scott saw no sense in memorizing place names—which in 1942 was a fairly sensible theory. Besides, it was the sort of warm spring day, with a touch of coolness in the breeze, which invited a boy to lie down in a field and stare at the occasional clouds till he fell asleep. Nuts to geography! Scott dozed.

About noon he got hungry, so his stocky legs carried him to a nearby store. There he invested his small hoard with penurious care and a sublime disregard for his gastric juices. He went down by the creek to feed.

Having finished his supply of cheese, chocolate, and cookies, and having drained the soda-pop bottle to its dregs, Scott caught tadpoles and studied them with a certain amount of scientific curiosity. He did not persevere. Something tumbled down the bank and thudded into the muddy ground near the water, so Scott, with a wary glance around, hurried to investigate.

It was a box. It was, in fact, the Box. The gadgetry hitched to it meant little to Scott, though he wondered why it was so fused and burnt. He pondered. With his jackknife he pried and probed, his tongue sticking out from a corner of his mouth—Hm-m-m. Nobody was around. Where had the box come from? Somebody must have left it here, and sliding soil had dislodged it from its precarious perch.

"That's a helix," Scott decided, quite erroneously. It was helical, but it wasn't a helix, because of the dimensional warp involved. Had the thing been a model airplane, no matter how complicated, it would have held few mysteries to Scott. As it was, a problem was posed. Something told Scott that the device was a lot more complicated than the spring motor he had deftly dismantled last Friday.

But no boy has ever left a box unopened, unless forcibly dragged away. Scott probed deeper. The angles on this thing were funny. Short circuit, probably. That was why—*uh!* The knife slipped. Scott sucked his thumb and gave vent to experienced blasphemy.

Maybe it was a music box.

Scott shouldn't have felt depressed. The gadgetry would have given Einstein a headache and driven Steinmetz raving mad. The trouble was, of course, that the box had not yet completely entered the space-time continuum where Scott existed, and therefore it could not be opened. At any rate, not till Scott used a convenient rock to hammer the helical non-helix into a more convenient position.

He hammered it, in fact, from its contact point with the fourth dimension, releasing the space-time torsion it had been maintaining. There was a brittle snap. The box jarred slightly, and lay motionless, no longer only partially in existence. Scott opened it easily now.

The soft, woven helmet was the first thing that caught his eye, but he discarded that without much interest. It was just a cap. Next he lifted a square, transparent crystal block, small enough to cup in his palm—much too small to contain the maze of apparatus within it. In a moment Scott had solved that problem. The crystal was a sort of magnifying glass, vastly enlarging the things inside the block. Strange things they were, too. Miniature people, for example—

They moved. Like clockwork automatons, though much more smoothly. It was rather like watching a play. Scott was interested in their costumes, but fascinated by their actions. The tiny people were deftly building a house. Scott wished it would catch fire, so he could see the people put it out.

Flames licked up from the half-completed structure. The automatons, with a great deal of odd apparatus, extinguished the blaze.

It didn't take Scott long to catch on. But he was a little worried. The manikins would obey his thoughts. By the time he discovered that, he was frightened, and threw the cube from him.

Halfway up the bank, he reconsidered and returned. The crystal block lay partly in the water, shining in the sun. It was a toy; Scott sensed that, with the unerring instinct of a child. But he didn't pick it up immediately. Instead, he returned to the box and investigated its remaining contents.

He found some really remarkable gadgets. The afternoon passed all too quickly. Scott finally put the toys back in the box and lugged it home, grunting and puffing. He was quite red-faced by the time he arrived at the kitchen door.

His find he hid at the back of a closet in his own room upstairs. The crystal cube he slipped into his pocket, which already bulged with string, a coil of wire, two pennies, a wad of tinfoil, a grimy defense stamp, and a chunk of feldspar. Emma, Scott's two-year-old sister, waddled unsteadily in from the hall and said hello.

"Hello, Slug," Scott nodded, from his altitude of seven years and some months. He patronized Emma shockingly, but she didn't know the difference. Small, plump, and wide-eyed, she flopped down on the carpet and stared dolefully at her shoes.

"Tie 'em, Scotty, please?"

"Sap," Scott told her kindly, but knotted the laces. "Dinner ready yet?" Emma nodded.

"Let's see your hands." For a wonder they were reasonably clean, though probably not aseptic. Scott regarded his own paws thoughtfully and, grimacing, went to the bathroom, where he made a sketchy toilet. The tadpoles had left traces.

Dennis Paradine and his wife Jane were having a cocktail before dinner, downstairs in the living room. He was a youngish, middle-aged man with gray-shot hair and a thinnish, prim-mouthed face; he taught philosophy at the university. Jane was small, neat, dark, and very pretty. She sipped her Martini and said:

"New shoes. Like 'em?"

"Here's to crime," Paradine muttered absently. "Huh? Shoes? Not now. Wait till I've finished this. I had a bad day."

"Exams?"

"Yeah. Flaming youth aspiring toward manhood. I hope they die. In considerable agony. *Insh'Allah!*"

"I want the olive," Jane requested.

"I know," Paradine said despondently. "It's been years since I've tasted one myself. In a Martini, I mean. Even if I put six of 'em in your glass, you're still not satisfied."

"I want yours. Blood brotherhood. Symbolism. That's why."

Paradine regarded his wife balefully and crossed his long legs. "You sound like one of my students."

"Like that hussy Betty Dawson, perhaps?" Jane unsheathed her nails. "Does she still leer at you in that offensive way?"

"She does. The child is a neat psychological problem. Luckily she isn't mine. If she were—" Paradine nodded significantly. "Sex consciousness and too many movies. I suppose she still thinks she can get a passing grade by showing me her knees. Which are, by the way, rather bony."

Jane adjusted her skirt with an air of complacent pride. Paradine uncoiled himself and poured fresh Martinis. "Candidly, I don't see the point of teaching those apes philosophy. They're all at the wrong age. Their habit-patterns, their methods of thinking, are already laid down.

They're horribly conservative, not that they'd admit it. The only people who can understand philosophy are mature adults or kids like Emma and Scotty."

"Well, don't enroll Scotty in your course," Jane requested. "He isn't ready to be a *Philosophiae Doctor*. I hold no brief for child geniuses, especially when it's my son."

"Scotty would probably be better at it than Betty Dawson," Paradine grunted.

"'He died an enfeebled old dotard at five,'" Jane quoted dreamily. "I want your olive."

"Here. By the way, I like the shoes."

"Thank you. Here's Rosalie. Dinner?"

"It's all ready, Miz Pa'dine," said Rosalie, hovering. "I'll call Miss Emma 'n' Mista' Scotty."

"I'll get 'em." Paradine put his head into the next room and roared, "Kids! Come and get it!"

Small feet scuttered down the stairs. Scott dashed into view, scrubbed and shining, a rebellious cowlick aimed at the zenith. Emma pursued, levering herself carefully down the steps. Halfway she gave up the attempt to descend upright and reversed, finishing the task monkey-fashion her small behind giving an impression of marvelous diligence upon the work in hand. Paradine watched, fascinated by the spectacle, till he was hurled back by the impact of his son's body.

"Hi, dad!" Scott shrieked.

Paradine recovered himself and regarded Scott with dignity. "Hi, yourself. Help me in to dinner. You've dislocated at least one of my hip joints."

But Scott was already tearing into the next room, where he stepped on Jane's new shoes in an ecstasy of affection, burbled an apology, and rushed off to find his place at the dinner table. Paradine cocked up an eyebrow as he followed, Emma's pudgy hand desperately gripping his forefinger.

"Wonder what the young devil's been up to?"

"No good, probably," Jane sighed. "Hello, darling. Let's see your ears."

"They're *clean*. Mickey licked 'em."

"Well, that Airedale's tongue is far cleaner than your ears," Jane pondered, making a brief examination. "Still, as long as you can hear, the dirt's only superficial."

"Fisshul?"

"Just a little, that means." Jane dragged her daughter to the table and inserted her legs into a high chair. Only lately had Emma graduated to the dignity of dining with the rest of the family, and she was, as Paradine remarked, all eat up with pride by the prospect. Only babies spilled food, Emma had been told. As a result, she took such painstaking care in conveying her spoon to her mouth that Paradine got the jitters whenever he watched.

"A conveyer belt would be the thing for Emma," he suggested, pulling out a chair for Jane. "Small buckets of spinach arriving at her face at stated intervals."

Dinner proceeded uneventfully until Paradine happened to glance at Scott's plate. "Hello, there. Sick? Been stuffing yourself at lunch?"

Scott thoughtfully examined the food still left before him. "I've had all I need, dad," he explained.

"You usually eat all you can hold, and a great deal more," Paradine said. "I know growing boys need several tons of foodstuff a day, but you're below par tonight. Feel O.K.?"

"Uh-huh. Honest, I've had all I need."

"All you *want?*"

"Sure. I eat different."

"Something they taught you at school?" Jane inquired.

Scott shook his head solemnly.

"Nobody taught me. I found it out myself. I use spit."

"Try again," Paradine suggested. "It's the wrong word."

"Uh . . . s-saliva. Hm-m-m?"

"Uh-huh. More pepsin? Is there pepsin in the salivary juices, Jane? I forget."

"There's poison in mine," Jane remarked. "Rosalie's left lumps in the mashed potatoes again."

But Paradine was interested. "You mean you're getting everything possible out of your food—no wastage—and eating less?"

Scott thought that over. "I guess so. It's not just the sp . . . saliva. I sort of measure how much to put in my mouth at once, and what stuff to mix up. I dunno. I just do it."

"Hm-m-m," said Paradine, making a note to check up later. "Rather a revolutionary idea." Kids often get screwy notions, but this one might not be so far off the beam. He pursed his lips. "Eventually I suppose people will eat quite differently—I mean the *way* they eat, as well as what. What they eat, I mean. Jane, our son shows signs of becoming a genius."

"Oh?"

"It's a rather good point in dietetics he just made. Did you figure it out yourself, Scott?"

"Sure," the boy said, and really believed it.

"Where'd you get the idea?"

"Oh, I—" Scott wriggled. "I dunno. It doesn't mean much, I guess."

Paradine was unreasonably disappointed. "But surely—"

"S-s-s-spit!" Emma shrieked, overcome by a sudden fit of badness. *"Spit!"* she attempted to demonstrate, but succeeded only in dribbling into her bib.

With a resigned air Jane rescued and reproved her daughter, while Paradine eyed Scott with rather puzzled interest. But it was not till after dinner, in the living room, that anything further happened.

"Any homework?"

"N-no," Scott said, flushing guiltily. To cover his embarrassment he took from his pocket a gadget he had found in the box, and began to unfold it. The result resembled a tesseract, strung with beads. Paradine didn't see it at first, but Emma did. She wanted to play with it.

"No. Lay off, Slug," Scott ordered. "You can watch me." He fumbled with the beads, making soft, interested noises. Emma extended a fat forefinger and yelped.

"Scotty," Paradine said warningly.

"I didn't hurt her."

"Bit me. It did," Emma mourned.

Paradine looked up. He frowned, staring. What in—

"Is that an abacus?" he asked. "Let's see it, please."

Somewhat unwillingly Scott brought the gadget across to his father's chair. Paradine blinked. The "abacus," unfolded, was more than a foot square, composed of thin, rigid wires that interlocked here and there. On the wires the colored beads were strung. They could be slid back and forth, and from one support to another, even at the points of jointure. But—a pierced bead couldn't cross *interlocking* wires—

So, apparently, they weren't pierced. Paradine looked closer. Each small sphere had a deep groove running around it, so that it could be revolved and slid along the wire at the same time. Paradine tried to pull one free. It clung as though magnetically. Iron? It looked more like plastic.

The framework itself—Paradine wasn't a mathematician. But the angles formed by the wires were vaguely shocking, in their ridiculous lack of Euclidean logic. They were a maze. Perhaps that's what the gadget was—a puzzle.

"Where'd you get this?"

"Uncle Harry gave it to me," Scott said on the spur of the moment. "Last Sunday, when he came over." Uncle Harry was out of town, a circumstance Scott well knew. At the age of seven, a boy soon learns that the vagaries of adults follow a certain definite pattern, and that they are fussy about the donors of gifts. Moreover, Uncle Harry would not return for several weeks; the expiration of that period was unimaginable to Scott, or, at least, the fact that his lie would ultimately be discovered meant less to him than the advantages of being allowed to keep the toy.

Paradine found himself growing slightly confused as he attempted to manipulate the beads. The angles were vaguely illogical. It was like a puzzle. This red bead, if slid along *this* wire to *that* junction, should reach *there*—but it didn't. A maze, odd, but no doubt instructive. Paradine had a well-founded feeling that he'd have no patience with the thing himself.

Scott did, however, retiring to a corner and sliding beads around with much fumbling and grunting. The beads *did* sting, when Scott chose the wrong ones or tried to slide them in the wrong direction. At last he crowed exultantly.

"I did it, dad!"

"Eh? What? Let's see." The device looked exactly the same to Paradine, but Scott pointed and beamed.

"I made it disappear."

"It's still there."

"That blue bead. It's gone now."

Paradine didn't believe that, so he merely snorted. Scott puzzled over the framework again. He experimented. This time there were no shocks, even slight. The abacus had showed him the correct method. Now it was up to him to do it on his own. The bizarre angles of the wires seemed a little less confusing now, somehow.

It was a most instructive toy—

It worked, Scott thought, rather like the crystal cube. Reminded of that gadget, he took it from his pocket and relinquished the abacus to Emma, who was struck dumb with joy. She fell to work sliding the beads, this time without protesting against the shocks—which, indeed, were very minor—and, being imitative, she managed to make a bead disappear almost as quickly as had Scott. The blue bead reappeared— but Scott didn't notice. He had forethoughtfully retired into an angle of the chesterfield with an overstuffed chair and amused himself with the cube.

There were little people inside the thing, tiny manikins much enlarged by the magnifying properties of the crystal, and they moved, all right. They built a house. It caught fire, with realistic-seeming flames, and stood by waiting. Scott puffed urgently. "Put it *out!*"

But nothing happened. Where was that queer fire engine, with revolving arms, that had appeared before? Here it was. It came sailing into the picture and stopped. Scott urged it on.

This was fun. Like putting on a play, only more real. The little people did what Scott told them, inside of his head. If he made a mistake, they waited till he'd found the right way. They even posed new problems for him—

The cube, too, was a most instructive toy. It was teaching Scott, with alarming rapidity—and teaching him very entertainingly. But it gave him no really new knowledge as yet. He wasn't ready. Later—later—

Emma grew tired of the abacus and went in search of Scott. She couldn't find him, even in his room, but once there the contents of the closet intrigued her. She discovered the box. It contained treasure-trove —a doll, which Scott had already noticed but discarded with a sneer. Squealing, Emma brought the doll downstairs, squatted in the middle of the floor, and began to take it apart.

"Darling! What's that?"

"Mr. Bear!"

Obviously it wasn't Mr. Bear, who was blind, earless, but comforting in his soft fatness. But all dolls were named Mr. Bear to Emma.

Jane Paradine hesitated. "Did you take that from some other little girl?"

"I didn't. She's mine."

Scott came out from his hiding place, thrusting the cube into his pocket. "Uh—that's from Uncle Harry."

"Did Uncle Harry give that to you, Emma?"

"He gave it to me for Emma," Scott put in hastily, adding another stone to his foundation of deceit. "Last Sunday."

"You'll break it, dear."

Emma brought the doll to her mother. "She comes apart. See?"

"Oh? It . . . *ugh!*" Jane sucked in her breath. Paradine looked up quickly.

"What's up?"

She brought the doll over to him, hesitated, and then went into the dining room, giving Paradine a significant glance. He followed, closing the door. Jane had already placed the doll on the cleared table.

"This isn't very nice, is it, Denny?"

"Hm-m-m." It was rather unpleasant, at first glance. One might have expected an anatomical dummy in a medical school, but a child's doll—

The thing came apart in sections, skin, muscles, organs, miniature but quite perfect, as far as Paradine could see. He was interested. "Dunno. Such things haven't the same connotations to a kid—"

"Look at that liver. Is it a liver?"

"Sure. Say, I . . . this is funny."

"What?"

"It isn't anatomically perfect, after all." Paradine pulled up a chair.

"The digestive tract's too short. No large intestine. No appendix, either."

"Should Emma have a thing like this?"

"I wouldn't mind having it myself," Paradine said. "Where on earth did Harry pick it up? No, I don't see any harm in it. Adults are conditioned to react unpleasantly to innards. Kids don't. They figure they're solid inside, like a potato. Emma can get a sound working knowledge of physiology from this doll."

"But what are those? Nerves?"

"No, these are the nerves. Arteries here; veins here. Funny sort of aorta—" Paradine looked baffled. "That . . . what's Latin for network? Anyway . . . huh? *Rita? Rata?*"

"*Rales,*" Jane suggested at random.

"That's a sort of breathing," Paradine said crushingly. "I can't figure out what this luminous network of stuff is. It goes all through the body, like nerves."

"Blood."

"Nope. Not circulatory, not neural—funny! It seems to be hooked up with the lungs."

They became engrossed, puzzling over the strange doll. It was made with remarkable perfection of detail, and that in itself was strange, in view of the physiological variation from the norm. "Wait'll I get that Gould," Paradine said, and presently was comparing the doll with anatomical charts. He learned little, except to increase his bafflement.

But it was more fun than a jigsaw puzzle.

Meanwhile, in the adjoining room, Emma was sliding the beads to and fro in the abacus. The motions didn't seem so strange now. Even when the beads vanished. She could almost follow that new direction—almost—

Scott panted, staring into the crystal cube and mentally directing, with many false starts, the building of a structure somewhat more complicated than the one which had been destroyed by fire. He, too, was learning—being conditioned—

Paradine's mistake, from a completely anthropomorphic standpoint, was that he didn't get rid of the toys instantly. He did not realize their significance, and, by the time he did, the progression of circumstances had got well under way. Uncle Harry remained out of town, so Paradine couldn't check with him. Too, the midterm exams were on, which meant arduous mental effort and complete exhaustion at night; and Jane was slightly ill for a week or so. Emma and Scott had free rein with the toys.

"What," Scott asked his father one evening, "is a wabe, dad?"

"Wave?"

He hesitated. "I . . . don't *think* so. Isn't wabe right?"

"Wab is Scot for web. That it?"

"I don't see how," Scott muttered, and wandered off, scowling, to amuse himself with the abacus. He was able to handle it quite deftly now. But, with the instinct of children for avoiding interruptions, he and Emma usually played with the toys in private. Not obviously, of course —but the more intricate experiments were never performed under the eye of an adult.

Scott was learning fast. What he now saw in the crystal cube had little relationship to the original simple problems. But they were fascinatingly technical. Had Scott realized that his education was being guided and supervised—though merely mechanically—he would probably have lost interest. As it was, his initiative was never quashed.

Abacus, cube, doll—and other toys the children found in the box—

Neither Paradine nor Jane guessed how much of an effect the contents of the time machine were having on the kids. How could they? Youngsters are instinctive dramatists, for purposes of self-protection. They have not yet fitted themselves to the exigencies—to them partially inexplicable—of a mature world. Moreover, their lives are complicated by human variables. They are told by one person that playing in the mud is permissible, but that, in their excavations, they must not uproot flowers or small trees. Another adult vetoes mud *per se*. The Ten Commandments are not carved on stone; they vary, and children are helplessly dependent on the caprice of those who give them birth and feed and clothe them. And tyrannize. The young animal does not resent that benevolent tyranny, for it is an essential part of nature. He is, however, an individualist, and maintains his integrity by a subtle, passive fight.

Under the eyes of an adult he changes. Like an actor on-stage, when he remembers, he strives to please, and also to attract attention to himself. Such attempts are not unknown to maturity. But adults are less obvious—to other adults.

It is difficult to admit that children lack subtlety. Children are different from the mature animal because they think in another way. We can more or less easily pierce the pretenses they set up—but they can do the same to us. Ruthlessly a child can destroy the pretenses of an adult. Iconoclasm is their prerogative.

Foppishness, for example. The amenities of social intercourse, exaggerated not quite to absurdity. The gigolo—

"Such *savoir faire!* Such punctilious courtesy!" The dowager and the blond young thing are often impressed. Men have less pleasant comments to make. But the child goes to the root of the matter.

"You're *silly!*"

How can an immature human understand the complicated system of social relationships? He can't. To him, an exaggeration of natural courtesy is silly. In his functional structure of life-patterns, it is rococo. He is an egotistic little animal, who cannot visualize himself in the position of another—certainly not an adult. A self-contained, almost perfect natural unit, his wants supplied by others, the child is much like a unicellular creature floating in the blood stream, nutriment carried to him, waste products carried away—

From the standpoint of logic, a child is rather horribly perfect. A baby may be even more perfect, but so alien to an adult that only superficial standards of comparison apply. The thought processes of an infant are completely unimaginable. But babies think, even before birth. In the womb they move and sleep, not entirely through instinct. We are conditioned to react rather peculiarly to the idea that a nearly-viable embryo may think. We are surprised, shocked into laughter, and repelled. Nothing human is alien.

But a baby is not human. An embryo is far less human.

That, perhaps, was why Emma learned more from the toys than did Scott. He could communicate his thoughts, of course; Emma could not, except in cryptic fragments. The matter of the scrawls, for example—

Give a young child pencil and paper, and he will draw something which looks different to him than to an adult. The absurd scribbles have little resemblance to a fire engine, but it *is* a fire engine, to a baby. Perhaps it is even three-dimensional. Babies think differently and see differently.

Paradine brooded over that, reading his paper one evening and watching Emma and Scott communicate. Scott was questioning his sister. Sometimes he did it in English. More often he had resource to gibberish and sign language. Emma tried to reply, but the handicap was too great.

Finally Scott got pencil and paper. Emma liked that. Tongue in cheek, she laboriously wrote a message. Scott took the paper, examined it, and scowled.

"That isn't right, Emma," he said.

Emma nodded vigorously. She seized the pencil again and made more scrawls. Scott puzzled for a while, finally smiled rather hesitantly, and got up. He vanished into the hall. Emma returned to the abacus.

Paradine rose and glanced down at the paper, with some mad thought that Emma might abruptly have mastered calligraphy. But she hadn't. The paper was covered with meaningless scrawls, of a type familiar to any parent. Paradine pursed his lips.

It might be a graph showing the mental variations of a manic-depressive cockroach, but probably wasn't. Still, it no doubt had meaning to Emma. Perhaps the scribble represented Mr. Bear.

Scott returned, looking pleased. He met Emma's gaze and nodded. Paradine felt a twinge of curiosity.

"Secrets?"

"Nope. Emma . . . uh . . . asked me to do something for her."

"Oh." Paradine, recalling instances of babies who had babbled in unknown tongues and baffled linguists, made a note to pocket the paper when the kids had finished with it. The next day he showed the scrawl to Elkins at the university. Elkins had a sound working knowledge of many unlikely languages, but he chuckled over Emma's venture into literature.

"Here's a free translation, Dennis. Quote. I don't know what this means, but I kid the hell out of my father with it. Unquote."

The two men laughed and went off to their classes. But later Paradine was to remember the incident. Especially after he met Holloway. Before that, however, months were to pass, and the situation to develop even further toward its climax.

Perhaps Paradine and Jane had evinced too much interest in the toys. Emma and Scott took to keeping them hidden, playing with them only in private. They never did it overtly, but with a certain unobtrusive caution. Nevertheless, Jane especially was somewhat troubled.

She spoke to Paradine about it one evening. "That doll Harry gave Emma."

"Yeah?"

"I was downtown today and tried to find out where it came from. No soap."

"Maybe Harry bought it in New York."

Jane was unconvinced. "I asked them about the other things, too. They showed me their stock—Johnsons's a big store, you know. But there's nothing like Emma's abacus."

"Hm-m-m." Paradine wasn't much interested. They had tickets for a show that night, and it was getting late. So the subject was dropped for the nonce.

Later it cropped up again, when a neighbor telephoned Jane.

"Scotty's never been like that, Denny. Mrs. Burns said he frightened the devil out of her Francis."

"Francis? A little fat bully of a punk, isn't he? Like his father. I broke Burns' nose for him once, when we were sophomores."

"Stop boasting and listen," Jane said, mixing a highball. "Scott showed Francis something that scared him. Hadn't you better—"

"I suppose so." Paradine listened. Noises in the next room told him the whereabouts of his son. "Scotty!"

"Bang," Scott said, and appeared smiling. "I killed 'em all. Space pirates. You want me, dad?"

"Yes. If you don't mind leaving the space pirates unburied for a few minutes. What did you do to Francis Burns?"

Scott's blue eyes reflected incredible candor. "Huh?"

"Try hard. You can remember, I'm sure."

"Uh. Oh, that. I didn't do nothing."

"Anything," Jane corrected absently.

"Anything. Honest. I just let him look into my television set, and it . . . it scared him."

"Television set?"

Scott produced the crystal cube. "It isn't really that. See?"

Paradine examined the gadget, startled by the magnification. All he could see, though, was a maze of meaningless colored designs.

"Uncle Harry—"

Paradine reached for the telephone. Scott gulped. "Is . . . is Uncle Harry back in town?"

"Yeah."

"Well, I gotta take a bath." Scott headed for the door. Paradine met Jane's gaze and nodded significantly.

Harry was home, but disclaimed all knowledge of the peculiar toys. Rather grimly, Paradine requested Scott to bring down from his room all of the playthings. Finally they lay in a row on the table, cube, abacus, doll, helmetlike cap, several other mysterious contraptions. Scott was cross-examined. He lied valiantly for a time, but broke down at last and bawled, hiccuping his confession.

"Get the box these things came in," Paradine ordered. "Then head for bed."

"Are you . . . *hup!* . . . gonna punish me, daddy?"

"For playing hooky and lying, yes. You know the rules. No more shows for two weeks. No sodas for the same period."

Scott gulped. "You gonna keep my things?"

"I don't know yet."

"Well . . . g'night, daddy. G'night, mom."

After the small figure had gone upstairs, Paradine dragged a chair to the table and carefully scrutinized the box. He poked thoughtfully at the fused gadgetry. Jane watched.

"What is it, Denny?"

"Dunno. Who'd leave a box of toys down by the creek?"

"It might have fallen out of a car."

"Not at that point. The road doesn't hit the creek north of the railroad trestle. Empty lots—nothing else." Paradine lit a cigarette. "Drink, honey?"

"I'll fix it." Jane went to work, her eyes troubled. She brought Paradine a glass and stood behind him, ruffling his hair with her fingers. "Is anything wrong?"

"Of course not. Only—where did these toys come from?"

"Johnsons's didn't know, and they get their stock from New York."

"I've been checking up, too," Paradine admitted. "That doll"—he poked it—"rather worried me. Custom jobs, maybe, but I wish I knew who'd made 'em."

"A psychologist? The abacus—don't they give people tests with such things?"

Paradine snapped his fingers. "Right! And say! There's a guy going to speak at the university next week, fellow named Holloway, who's a child psychologist. He's a big shot, with quite a reputation. He might know something about it."

"Holloway? I don't—"

"Rex Holloway. He's . . . hm-m-m! He doesn't live far from here. Do you suppose he might have had these things made himself?"

Jane was examining the abacus. She grimaced and drew back. "If he did, I don't like him. But see if you can find out, Denny."

Paradine nodded. "I shall."

He drank his highball, frowning. He was vaguely worried. But he wasn't scared—yet.

Rex Holloway was a fat, shiny man, with a bald head and thick spectacles, above which his thick, black brows lay like bushy caterpillars. Paradine brought him home to dinner one night a week later. Holloway did not appear to watch the children, but nothing they did or said was lost on him. His gray eyes, shrewd and bright, missed little.

The toys fascinated him. In the living room the three adults gathered around the table, where the playthings had been placed. Holloway studied them carefully as he listened to what Jane and Paradine had to say. At last he broke his silence.

"I'm glad I came here tonight. But not completely. This is very disturbing, you know."

"Eh?" Paradine stared, and Jane's face showed her consternation. Holloway's next words did not calm them.

"We are dealing with madness."

He smiled at the shocked looks they gave him. "All children are mad, from an adult viewpoint. Ever read Hughes' 'High Wind in Jamaica'?"

"I've got it." Paradine secured the little book from its shelf. Holloway extended a hand, took it, and flipped the pages till he had found the place he wanted. He read aloud:

" 'Babies of course are not human—they are animals, and have a very ancient and ramified culture, as cats have, and fishes, and even snakes; the same in kind as these, but much more complicated and vivid, since babies are, after all, one of the most developed species of the lower vertebrates. In short, babies have minds which work in terms and categories of their own which cannot be translated into the terms and categories of the human mind.' "

Jane tried to take that calmly, but couldn't. "You don't mean that Emma—"

"Could you think like your daughter?" Holloway asked. "Listen: 'One can no more think like a baby than one can think like a bee.' "

Paradine mixed drinks. Over his shoulder he said, "You're theorizing quite a bit, aren't you? As I get it, you're implying that babies have a culture of their own, even a high standard of intelligence."

"Not necessarily. There's no yardstick, you see. All I say is that babies think in other ways than we do. Not necessarily *better*—that's a question of relative values. But with a different manner of extension—" He sought for words, grimacing.

"Fantasy," Paradine said, rather rudely, but annoyed because of Emma. "Babies don't have different senses from ours."

"Who said they did?" Holloway demanded. "They use their minds in a different way, that's all. But it's quite enough!"

"I'm trying to understand," Jane said slowly. "All I can think of is my Mixmaster. It can whip up batter and potatoes, but it can squeeze oranges, too."

"Something like that. The brain's a colloid, a very complicated machine. We don't know much about its potentialities. We don't even know how much it can grasp. But it *is* known that the mind becomes conditioned as the human animal matures. It follows certain familiar theorems, and all thought thereafter is pretty well based on patterns taken for granted. Look at this." Holloway touched the abacus. "Have you experimented with it?"

"A little," Paradine said.

"But not much. Eh?"

"Well—"

"Why not?"

"It's pointless," Paradine complained. "Even a puzzle has to have some logic. But those crazy angles—"

"Your mind has been conditioned to Euclid," Holloway said. "So this—thing—bores us, and seems pointless. But a child knows nothing of Euclid. A different sort of geometry from ours wouldn't impress him as being illogical. He believes what he sees."

"Are you trying to tell me that this gadget's got a fourth-dimensional extension?" Paradine demanded.

"Not visually, anyway," Holloway denied. "All I say is that our minds, conditioned to Euclid, can see nothing in this but an illogical tangle of wires. But a child—especially a baby—might see more. Not at first. It'd be a puzzle, of course. Only a child wouldn't be handicapped by too many preconceived ideas."

"Hardening of the thought-arteries," Jane interjected.

Paradine was not convinced. "Then a baby could work calculus better than Einstein? No, I don't mean that. I can see your point, more or less clearly. Only—"

"Well, look. Let's suppose there are two kinds of geometry—we'll limit it, for the sake of the example. Our kind, Euclidean, and another, which we'll call x. X hasn't much relationship to Euclid. It's based on different theorems. Two and two needn't equal four in it; they could equal y_2, or they might not even *equal*. A baby's mind is not yet conditioned, except by certain questionable factors of heredity and environment. Start the infant on Euclid—"

"Poor kid," Jane said.

Holloway shot her a quick glance. "The basis of Euclid. Alphabet blocks. Math, geometry, algebra—they come much later. We're familiar with that development. On the other hand, start the baby with the basic principles of our x logic."

"Blocks? What kind?"

Holloway looked at the abacus. "It wouldn't make much sense to us. But we've been conditioned to Euclid."

Paradine poured himself a stiff shot of whiskey. "That's pretty awful. You're not limiting to math."

"Right! I'm not limiting it at all. How can I? I'm not conditioned to x logic."

"There's the answer," Jane said, with a sigh of relief. "Who is? It'd take such a person to make the sort of toys you apparently think these are."

Holloway nodded, his eyes, behind the thick lenses, blinking. "Such people may exist."

"Where?"

"They might prefer to keep hidden."

"Supermen?"

"I wish I knew. You see, Paradine, we've got yardstick trouble again. By our standards these people might seem super-doopers in certain respects. In others they might seem moronic. It's not a quantitative difference; it's qualitative. They *think* different. And I'm sure we can do things they can't."

"Maybe they wouldn't want to," Jane said.

Paradine tapped the fused gadgetry on the box. "What about this? It implies—"

"A purpose, sure."

"Transportation?"

"One thinks of that first. If so, the box might have come from anywhere."

"Where—things are—*different?*" Paradine asked slowly.

"Exactly. In space, or even time. I don't know; I'm a pyschologist. Unfortunately I'm conditioned to Euclid, too."

"Funny place it must be," Jane said. "Denny, get rid of those toys."

"I intend to."

Holloway picked up the crystal cube. "Did you question the children much?"

Paradine said, "Yeah. Scott said there were people in that cube when he first looked. I asked him what was in it now."

"What did he say?" The psychologist's eyes widened.

"He said they were building a place. His exact words. I asked him who—people? But he couldn't explain."

"No, I suppose not," Holloway muttered. "It must be progressive. How long have the children had these toys?"

"About three months, I guess."

"Time enough. The perfect toy, you see, is both instructive and mechanical. It should do things, to interest a child, and it should teach, preferably unobtrusively. Simple problems at first. Later—"

"*X* logic," Jane said, white-faced.

Paradine cursed under his breath. "Emma and Scott are perfectly normal!"

"Do you know how their minds work—now?"

Holloway didn't pursue the thought. He fingered the doll. "It would be interesting to know the conditions of the place where these things came from. Induction doesn't help a great deal, though. Too many factors are missing. We can't visualize a world based on the *x* factor—environment adjusted to minds thinking in *x* patterns. This luminous network inside the doll. It could be anything. It could exist inside us, though we haven't discovered it yet. When we find the right stain—" He shrugged. "What do you make of this?"

It was a crimson globe, two inches in diameter, with a protruding knob upon its surface.

"What could anyone make of it?"

"Scott? Emma?"

"I hadn't even seen it till about three weeks ago. Then Emma started to play with it." Paradine nibbled his lip. "After that, Scott got interested."

"Just what do they do?"

"Hold it up in front of them and move it back and forth. No particular pattern of motion."

"No Euclidean pattern," Holloway corrected. "At first they couldn't understand the toy's purpose. They had to be educated up to it."

"That's horrible," Jane said.

"Not to them. Emma is probably quicker at understanding x than is Scott, for her mind isn't yet conditioned to this environment."

Paradine said, "But I can remember plenty of things I did as a child. Even as a baby."

"Well?"

"Was I—mad—then?"

"The things you don't remember are the criterion of your madness," Holloway retorted. "But I use the word 'madness' purely as a convenient symbol for the variation from the known human norm. The arbitrary standard of sanity."

Jane put down her glass. "You've said that induction was difficult, Mr. Holloway. But it seems to me you're making a great deal of it from very little. After all, these toys—"

"I *am* a psychologist, and I've specialized in children. I'm not a layman. These toys mean a great deal to me, chiefly because they mean so little."

"You might be wrong."

"Well, I rather hope I am. I'd like to examine the children."

Jane rose in arms. "How?"

After Holloway had explained, she nodded, though still a bit hesitantly. "Well, that's all right. But they're not guinea pigs."

The psychologist patted the air with a plump hand. "My dear girl! I'm not a Frankenstein. To me the individual is the prime factor— naturally, since I work with minds. If there's anything wrong with the youngsters, I want to cure them."

Paradine put down his cigarette and slowly watched blue smoke spiral up, wavering in an unfelt draft. "Can you give a prognosis?"

"I'll try. That's all I can say. If the undeveloped minds have been turned into the x channel, it's necessary to divert them back. I'm not saying that's the wisest thing to do, but it probably is from our standards. After all, Emma and Scott will have to live in this world."

"Yeah. Yeah. I can't believe there's much wrong. They seem about average, thoroughly normal."

"Superficially they may seem so. They've no reason for acting abnormally, have they? And how can you tell if they—think differently?"

"I'll call 'em," Paradine said.

"Make it informal, then. I don't want them to be on guard."

Jane nodded toward the toys. Holloway said, "Leave the stuff there, eh?"

But the psychologist, after Emma and Scott were summoned, made no immediate move at direct questioning. He managed to draw Scott unobtrusively into the conversation, dropping key words now and then. Nothing so obvious as a word-association test—co-operation is necessary for that.

The most interesting development occurred when Holloway took up the abacus. "Mind showing me how this works?"

Scott hesitated. "Yes, sir. Like this—" He slid a bead deftly through the maze, in a tangled course, so swiftly that no one was quite sure whether or not it ultimately vanished. It might have been merely legerdemain. Then, again—

Holloway tried. Scott watched, wrinkling his nose.

"That right?"

"Uh-huh. It's gotta go *there*—"

"Here? Why?"

"Well, that's the only way to make it work."

But Holloway was conditioned to Euclid. There was no apparent reason why the bead should slide from this particular wire to the other. It looked like a random factor. Also, Holloway suddenly noticed, this wasn't the path the bead had taken previously, when Scott had worked the puzzle. At least, as well as he could tell.

"Will you show me again?"

Scott did, and twice more, on request. Holloway blinked through his glasses. Random, yes. And a variable. Scott moved the bead along a different course each time.

Somehow, none of the adults could tell whether or not the bead vanished. If they had expected to see it disappear, their reactions might have been different.

In the end nothing was solved. Holloway, as he said good night, seemed ill at ease.

"May I come again?"

"I wish you would," Jane told him. "Any time. You still think—"

He nodded. "The children's minds are not reacting normally. They're not dull at all, but I've the most extraordinary impression that they arrive at conclusions in a way we don't understand. As though they used algebra while we used geometry. The same conclusion, but a different method of reaching it."

"What about the toys?" Paradine asked suddenly.

"Keep them out of the way. I'd like to borrow them, if I may—"

That night Paradine slept badly. Holloway's parallel had been ill-chosen. It led to disturbing theories. The x factor—The children were using the equivalent of algebraic reasoning, while adults used geometry.

Fair enough. Only—

Algebra can give you answers that geometry cannot, since there are certain terms and symbols which cannot be expressed geometrically. Suppose x logic showed conclusions inconceivable to an adult mind?

"Damn!" Paradine whispered. Jane stirred beside him.

"Dear? Can't you sleep either?"

"No." He got up and went into the next room. Emma slept peacefully as a cherub, her fat arm curled around Mr. Bear. Through the open doorway Paradine could see Scott's dark head motionless on the pillow.

Jane was beside him. He slipped his arm around her.

"Poor little people," she murmured. "And Holloway called them mad. I think we're the ones who are crazy, Dennis."

"Uh-huh. We've got jitters."

Scott stirred in his sleep. Without awakening, he called what was obviously a question, though it did not seem to be in any particular language. Emma gave a little mewling cry that changed pitch sharply.

She had not wakened. The children lay without stirring.

But Paradine thought, with a sudden sickness in his middle, it was exactly as though Scott had asked Emma something, and she had replied.

Had their minds changed so that even—sleep—was different to them?

He thrust the thought away. "You'll catch cold. Let's get back to bed. Want a drink?"

"I think I do," Jane said, watching Emma. Her hand reached out blindly toward the child; she drew it back. "Come on. We'll wake the kids."

They drank a little brandy together, but said nothing. Jane cried in her sleep, later.

Scott was not awake, but his mind worked in slow, careful building. Thus—

"They'll take the toys away. The fat man . . . listava dangerous maybe. But the Ghoric direction won't show . . . evankrus dun-hasn't-them. Intransdection . . . bright and shiny. Emma. She's more kho-pranik-high now than . . . I still don't see how to . . . thavarar lixery dist—"

A little of Scott's thoughts could still be understood. But Emma had become conditioned to x much faster.

She was thinking, too.

Not like an adult or a child. Not even like a human. Except, perhaps, a human of a type shockingly unfamiliar to *genus homo*.

Sometimes Scott himself had difficulty in following her thoughts.

If it had not been for Holloway, life might have settled back into an almost normal routine. The toys were no longer active reminders. Emma still enjoyed her dolls and sand pile, with a thoroughly explicable delight. Scott was satisfied with baseball and his chemical set. They did everything other children did, and evinced few, if any, flashes of abnormality. But Holloway seemed to be an alarmist.

He was having the toys tested, with rather idiotic results. He drew endless charts and diagrams, corresponded with mathematicians, engineers, and other psychologists, and went quietly crazy trying to find rhyme or reason in the construction of the gadgets. The box itself, with its cryptic machinery, told nothing. Fusing had melted too much of the stuff into slag. But the toys—

It was the random element that baffled investigation. Even that was a matter of semantics. For Holloway was convinced that it wasn't really random. There just weren't enough known factors. No adult could work the abacus, for example. And Holloway thoughtfully refrained from letting a child play with the thing.

The crystal cube was similarly cryptic. It showed a mad pattern of colors, which sometimes moved. In this it resembled a kaleidoscope. But the shifting of balance and gravity didn't affect it. Again the random factor.

Or, rather, the unknown. The x pattern. Eventually Paradine and Jane slipped back into something like complacence, with a feeling that the children had been cured of their mental quirk, now that the contributing cause had been removed. Certain of the actions of Emma and Scott gave them every reason to quit worrying.

For the kids enjoyed swimming, hiking, movies, games, the normal functional toys of this particular time-sector. It was true that they failed to master certain rather puzzling mechanical devices which involved some calculation. A three-dimensional jigsaw globe Paradine had picked up, for example. But he found that difficult himself.

Once in a while there were lapses. Scott was hiking with his father one Saturday afternoon, and the two had paused at the summit of a hill. Beneath them a rather lovely valley was spread.

"Pretty, isn't it?" Paradine remarked.

Scott examined the scene gravely. "It's all wrong," he said.

"Eh?"

"I dunno."

"What's wrong about it?"

"Gee—" Scott lapsed into puzzled silence. "I dunno."

The children had missed their toys, but not for long. Emma recovered first, though Scott still moped. He held unintelligible conversations with his sister, and studied meaningless scrawls she drew on paper he supplied. It was almost as though he was consulting her, anent difficult problems beyond his grasp.

If Emma understood more, Scott had more real intelligence, and manipulatory skill as well. He built a gadget with his Meccano set, but was dissatisfied. The apparent cause of his dissatisfaction was exactly why Paradine was relieved when he viewed the structure. It was the sort of thing a normal boy would make, vaguely reminiscent of a cubistic ship.

It was a bit too normal to please Scott. He asked Emma more questions, though in private. She thought for a time, and then made more scrawls with an awkwardly clutched pencil.

"Can you read that stuff?" Jane asked her son one morning.

"Not read it, exactly. I can tell what she means. Not all the time, but mostly."

"Is it writing?"

"N-no. It doesn't mean what it *looks* like."

"Symbolism," Paradine suggested over his coffee.

Jane looked at him, her eyes widening. "Denny—"

He winked and shook his head. Later, when they were alone, he said, "Don't let Holloway upset you. I'm not implying that the kids are corresponding in an unknown tongue. If Emma draws a squiggle and says it's a flower, that's an arbitrary rule—Scott remembers that. Next time she draws the same sort of squiggle, or tries to—well!"

"Sure," Jane said doubtfully. "Have you noticed Scott's been doing a lot of reading lately?"

"I noticed. Nothing unusual, though. No Kant or Spinoza."

"He browses, that's all."

"Well, so did I, at his age," Paradine said, and went off to his morning classes. He lunched with Holloway, which was becoming a daily habit, and spoke of Emma's literary endeavors.

"Was I right about symbolism, Rex?"

The psychologist nodded. "Quite right. Our own language is nothing but arbitrary symbolism now. At least in its application. Look here." On his napkin he drew a very narrow ellipse. "What's that?"

"You mean what does it represent?"

"Yes. What does it suggest to you? It could be a crude representation of—what?"

"Plenty of things," Paradine said. "Rim of a glass. A fried egg. A loaf of French bread. A cigar."

Holloway added a little triangle to his drawing, apex joined to one end of the ellipse. He looked up at Paradine.

"A fish," the latter said instantly.

"Our familiar symbol for a fish. Even without fins, eyes or mouth, it's recognizable, because we've been conditioned to identify this particular shape with our mental picture of a fish. The basis of a rebus. A symbol, to us, means a lot more than what we actually see on paper. What's in your mind when you look at this sketch?"

"Why—a fish."

"Keep going. What do you visualize—everything!"

"Scales," Paradine said slowly, looking into space. "Water. Foam. A fish's eye. The fins. The colors."

"So the symbol represents a lot more than just the abstract idea *fish*. Note the connotation's that of a noun, not a verb. It's harder to express actions by symbolism, you know. Anyway—reverse the process. Suppose you want to make a symbol for some concrete noun, say *bird*. Draw it."

Paradine drew two connected arcs, concavities down.

"The lowest common denominator," Holloway nodded. "The natural tendency is to simplify. Especially when a child is seeing something for the first time and has few standards of comparison. He tries to identify the new thing with what's already familiar to him. Ever notice how a child draws the ocean?" He didn't wait for an answer; he went on.

"A series of jagged points. Like the oscillating line on a seismograph. When I first saw the Pacific, I was about three. I remember it pretty clearly. It looked—tilted. A flat plain, slanted at an angle. The waves were regular triangles, apex upward. Now I didn't *see* them stylized that way, but later, remembering, I had to find some familiar standard of comparison. Which is the only way of getting any conception of an entirely new thing. The average child tries to draw these regular triangles, but his co-ordination's poor. He gets a seismograph pattern."

"All of which means. what?"

"A child sees the ocean. He stylizes it. He draws a certain definite pattern, symbolic, to him, of the sea. Emma's scrawls may be symbols, too. I don't mean that the world looks different to her—brighter, perhaps, and sharper, more vivid and with a slackening of perception above her eye level. What I do mean is that her thought-processes are different, that she translates what she sees into abnormal symbols."

"You still believe—"

"Yes, I do. Her mind has been conditioned unusually. It may be that she breaks down what she sees into simple, obvious patterns—and realizes a significance to those patterns that we can't understand. Like the abacus. She saw a pattern in that, though to us it was completely random."

Paradine abruptly decided to taper off these luncheon engagements with Holloway. The man was an alarmist. His theories were growing more fantastic than ever, and he dragged in anything, applicable or not, that would support them.

Rather sardonically he said, "Do you mean Emma's communicating with Scott in an unknown language?"

"In symbols for which she hasn't any words. I'm sure Scott understands a great deal of those—scrawls. To him, an isosceles triangle may represent any factor, though probably a concrete noun. Would a man who knew nothing of algebra understand what H_2O meant? Would he realize that the symbol could evoke a picture of the ocean?"

Paradine didn't answer. Instead, he mentioned to Holloway Scott's curious remark that the landscape, from the hill, had looked all wrong. A moment later, he was inclined to regret his impulse, for the psychologist was off again.

"Scott's thought-patterns are building up to a sum that doesn't equal this world. Perhaps he's subconsciously expecting to see the world where those toys came from."

Paradine stopped listening. Enough was enough. The kids were getting along all right, and the only remaining disturbing factor was Holloway himself. That night, however, Scott evinced an interest, later significant, in eels.

There was nothing apparently harmful in natural history. Paradine explained about eels.

"But where do they lay their eggs? Or do they?"

"That's still a mystery. Their spawning grounds are unknown. Maybe the Sargasso Sea, or the deeps, where the pressure can help them force the young out of their bodies."

"Funny," Scott said, thinking deeply.

"Salmon do the same thing, more or less. They go up rivers to spawn." Paradine went into detail. Scott was fascinated.

"But that's *right,* dad. They're born in the river, and when they learn how to swim, they go down to the sea. And they come back to lay their eggs, huh?"

"Right."

"Only they wouldn't *come* back," Scott pondered. "They'd just send their eggs—"

"It'd take a very long ovipositor," Paradine said, and vouchsafed some well-chosen remarks upon oviparity.

His son wasn't entirely satisfied. Flowers, he contended, sent their seeds long distances.

"They don't guide them. Not many find fertile soil."

"Flowers haven't got brains, though. Dad, why do people live *here?*"

"Glendale?"

"No—*here.* This whole place. It isn't all there is, I bet."

"Do you mean the other planets?"

Scott was hesitant. "This is only—part—of the big place. It's like the river where the salmon go. Why don't people go on down to the ocean when they grow up?"

Paradine realized that Scott was speaking figuratively. He felt a brief chill. The—ocean?

The young of the species are not conditioned to live in the completer world of their parents. Having developed sufficiently, they enter that world. Later they breed. The fertilized eggs are buried in the sand, far up the river, where later they hatch.

And they learn. Instinct alone is fatally slow. Especially in the case of a specialized genus, unable to cope even with this world, unable to feed or drink or survive, unless someone has foresightedly provided for those needs.

The young, fed and tended, would survive. There would be incubators and robots. They would survive, but they would not know how to swim downstream, to the vaster world of the ocean.

So they must be taught. They must be trained and conditioned in many ways.

Painlessly, subtly, unobtrusively. Children love toys that do things— and if those toys teach at the same time—

In the latter half of the nineteenth century an Englishman sat on a grassy bank near a stream. A very small girl lay near him, staring up at the sky. She had discarded a curious toy with which she had been playing, and now was murmuring a wordless little song, to which the man listened with half an ear.

"What was that, my dear?" he asked at last.

"Just something I made up, Uncle Charles."

"Sing it again." He pulled out a notebook.

The girl obeyed.

"Does it mean anything?"

She nodded. "Oh, yes. Like the stories I tell you, you know."

"They're wonderful stories, dear."

"And you'll put them in a book some day?"

"Yes, but I must change them quite a lot, or no one would understand. But I don't think I'll change your little song."

"You mustn't. If you did, it wouldn't mean anything."

"I won't change that stanza, anyway," he promised. "Just what does it mean?"

"It's the way out, I think," the girl said doubtfully. "I'm not sure yet. My magic toys told me."

"I wish I knew what London shop sold those marvelous toys!"

"Mamma bought them for me. She's dead. Papa doesn't care."

She lied. She had found the toys in a box one day, as she played by the Thames. And they were indeed wonderful.

Her little song—Uncle Charles thought it didn't mean anything. (He wasn't her real uncle, she parenthesized. But he was nice.) The song meant a great deal. It was the way. Presently she would do what it said, and then—

But she was already too old. She never found the way.

Paradine had dropped Holloway. Jane had taken a dislike to him, naturally enough, since what she wanted most of all was to have her fears calmed. Since Scott and Emma acted normally now, Jane felt satisfied. It was partly wishful-thinking, to which Paradine could not entirely subscribe.

Scott kept bringing gadgets to Emma for her approval. Usually she'd shake her head. Sometimes she would look doubtful. Very occasionally she would signify agreement. Then there would be an hour of laborious, crazy scribbling on scraps of note paper, and Scott, after studying the notations, would arrange and rearrange his rocks, bits of machinery, candle ends, and assorted junk. Each day the maid cleaned them away, and each day Scott began again.

He condescended to explain a little to his puzzled father, who could see no rhyme or reason in the game.

"But why this pebble right here?"

"It's hard and round, dad. It *belongs* there."

"So is this one hard and round."

"Well, that's got vaseline on it. When you get that far, you can't *see* just a hard round thing."

"What comes next? This candle?"

Scott looked disgusted. "That's toward the end. The iron ring's next."

It was, Paradine thought, like a Scout trail through the woods, markers in a labyrinth. But here again was the random factor. Logic halted— familiar logic—at Scott's motives in arranging the junk as he did.

Paradine went out. Over his shoulder he saw Scott pull a crumpled piece of paper and a pencil from his pocket, and head for Emma, who was squatted in a corner thinking things over.

Well—

Jane was lunching with Uncle Harry, and, on this hot Sunday afternoon there was little to do but read the papers. Paradine settled himself in the coolest place he could find, with a Collins, and lost himself in the comic strips.

An hour later a clatter of feet upstairs roused him from his doze. Scott's voice was crying exultantly, "This is it, Slug! Come on—"

Paradine stood up quickly, frowning. As he went into the hall the telephone began to ring. Jane had promised to call—

His hand was on the receiver when Emma's faint voice squealed with excitement. Paradine grimaced. What the devil was going on upstairs?

Scott shrieked, "Look out! This way!"

Paradine, his mouth working, his nerves ridiculously tense, forgot the phone and raced up the stairs. The door of Scott's room was open.

The children were vanishing.

They went in fragments, like thick smoke in a wind, or like movement in a distorting mirror. Hand in hand they went, in a direction Paradine could not understand, and as he blinked there on the threshold, they were gone.

"Emma!" he said, dry-throated. *"Scotty!"*

On the carpet lay a pattern of markers, pebbles, an iron ring—junk. A random pattern. A crumpled sheet of paper blew toward Paradine.

He picked it up automatically.

"Kids. Where are you? Don't hide—

"Emma! SCOTTY!"

Downstairs the telephone stopped its shrill, monotonous ringing. Paradine looked at the paper he held.

It was a leaf torn from a book. There were interlineations and marginal notes, in Emma's meaningless scrawl. A stanza of verse had been so underlined and scribbled over that it was almost illegible, but Paradine was thoroughly familiar with "Through the Looking Glass." His memory gave him the words—

> 'Twas brillig, and the slithy toves
>   Did gyre and gimbel in the wabe.
> All mimsy were the borogoves,
>   And the mome raths outgrabe.

Idiotically he thought: Humpty Dumpty explained it. A wabe is the plot of grass around a sundial. A sundial. Time—It has something to do with time. A long time ago Scotty asked me what a wabe was. Symbolism.

'Twas brillig—

A perfect mathematical formula, giving all the conditions, in symbolism the children had finally understood. The junk on the floor. The toves had to be made slithy—vaseline?—and they had to be placed in a certain relationship, so that they'd gyre and gimbel.

Lunacy!

But it had not been lunacy to Emma and Scott. They thought differently. They used *x* logic. Those notes Emma had made on the page—she'd translated Carroll's words into symbols both she and Scott could understand.

The random factor had made sense to the children. They had fulfilled the conditions of the time-space equation. *And the mome raths outgrabe—*

Paradine made a rather ghastly little sound, deep in his throat. He looked at the crazy pattern on the carpet. If he could follow it, as the kids had done— But he couldn't. The pattern was senseless. The random factor defeated him. He was conditioned to Euclid.

Even if he went insane, he still couldn't do it. It would be the wrong kind of lunacy.

His mind had stopped working now. But in a moment the stasis of incredulous horror would pass— Paradine crumpled the page in his fingers. "Emma, Scotty," he called in a dead voice, as though he could expect no response.

Sunlight slanted through the open windows, brightening the golden pelt of Mr. Bear. Downstairs the ringing of the telephone began again.

*   *   *

According to the story, what does the learning process consist of? That is, how does a human being go about learning in order to become what we understand as human? And how is language important to this process? What is meant by such terms as "*x* patterns" or "*x* logic"? How about a term like "conditioned to Euclid"? Can you see any justification for Padgett's use of Lewis Carroll in the story? (It is assumed you will know who Lewis Carroll was.)

But the story is built on the possibility that the whole process of this learning as we know and accept it may obscure something. Obscure what?

The story is science fiction, a fantasy. And yet it has been said of fantasy that one of its functions is to make you resee the familiar from a new angle, to recover a freshness of vision the effect of which is to cause you to realize that all you thought "you had (or knew) was dangerous and potent, not really effectively chained [but] free and wild; no more yours than [it was] you" (J. R. R. Tolkien, "On Fairy-Stories"). William J. J. Gordon puts it this way:

> To break through toward a creative act, it is necessary to twist out of phase whatever conventional laws appear to hold. This does not mean that it is necessary to defy all the basic hypotheses of our phenomenology, but that it is necessary to defy them *apparently*. Then, through the cracks which appear when the laws are twisted out of phase (all this attained through conscious self-deceit), things can be seen in a new way. So long as the rules are accepted as immutable "laws of vision" the world always will appear to be the same and no novelties can be discovered or fabricated. Many highly trained people naturally tend to think in terms of the dogma of their own technology and it frightens them to twist their conventions out of phase. Their conventions sometimes constitute a background of knowledge upon which they rely for their emotional stability. Such experts do not want cracks to appear. They identify their psychic order with the cosmic order and any cracks are signs of their orderly cosmos breaking up.
>
> *—William J. J. Gordon* *

How does Padgett's story enable you to see the process of education —specifically its benefits and liabilities—in a new way, from a new angle?

Commentary

I'll begin by asking the class to prepare Assignment 26 for a discussion for the next period. I'll also have the students write a paper addressing Assignment 27 which will be due that same period. Once again I will use a five minute written quiz to find out which students have looked up Lewis Carroll.

* * *

As literature there's no question that the Padgett story is a pretty crude piece of work (that husband and wife dialogue, the domestic scenes in general, are particularly painful to read), but I'm not going to deal with the story this way in class (which I'll more than make up for with *The Willowdale Handcar*), because I have a feeling that with it a number of students are going to be able to place a great many of the matters we've been considering with a surety that up to this point they

* From pp. 96, 127, and 128 in *Synectics,* by William J. J. Gordon. Copyright © 1961 by William J. J. Gordon. By permission of Harper & Row, Publishers, Inc.

just haven't had. At any rate, Padgett's having Scotty and Emma make use of educational toys (specifically) to develop a language (literally) which enables them to pass bodily (and permanently) into another world, is a very clear dramatization of the way in which language may be said to be related to the process of teaching and learning and of the way also in which the learning process may be said to involve a change in seeing which is a change in who and where one is. In addition, I think that the story will introduce a new and very necessary dimension ("a new angle" from which to "resee the familiar") to the highly celebrative talk about good learning which has begun to characterize a number of my more recent classes—talk which seems to suggest that the process is one we can all take for granted as unequivocally beneficial (it's to the possibilities of more complicated ways of talking that the final question of the assignment, as well as the quotations from Gordon and Tolkien, are intended to lead the students).

There is no mistaking that at whatever human level there is to the story, the emphasis falls more on Paradine's loss as a father than it does on the gain of Scotty and Emma—and this in spite of the implication that the children have "found the way," gone "down to the ocean," because they've grown up. I don't know whether that final moment in the story with the irrelevantly ringing telephone and the teddy bear in the sun can have the poignance for someone who has never experienced being a parent that it has for me, but I can't see myself having much trouble generating a conversation in class toward the end of the period over how education can make one a stranger to other things in his life. (What is home like that first Thanksgiving vacation? Or the Christmas holiday you push for and dream of all fall—are the reunitings exactly what you thought they would be?)

Partly to prepare the students for *The Willowdale Handcar* but also to make sure that they understand how Padgett makes artistic use of the relation of language to experience, I'll spend some time (in fact I think I'll begin class this way) with his use of Lewis Carroll. I don't think that the students will need help with the plot part of it, understanding that Alice is the recipient of the first Box Unthahorsten sent back in time. Nor, if they've looked up Lewis Carroll, should they have much difficulty realizing that "Uncle Charles" is Charles Dodgson and "the small girl" Alice Liddell. Even the information in an encyclopedia should help them work out that Padgett is using Alice as Dodgson's source for *Alice in Wonderland* and *Alice Through the Looking Glass*. Carroll's nonsense, then, according to Padgett, is only a modified version of what Alice has repeated to him from what her "magic toys" (out of Unthahorsten's Box) have told her. "Jabberwocky," which "Uncle Charles" promises to print just the way Alice recites it to him, is actually a mathematical formula for leaving this dimension of time and space for another—a formula which Scotty and Emma (who are not, as Alice is, "too old," too Euclideanly oriented, to do it) work out and act on with the help of *their* magic toys, thereby finding "the way" to pass from this world to another.

What I think the students may have trouble understanding, however, is the aptness of Padgett's use of Lewis Carroll, or more specifically of Carroll's classic writings of nonsense. I'll talk about this a bit because I think I can use Padgett's use of nonsense as a way of getting to what I'd call the most important effect of the story, what the story as a fantasy enables me to resee: namely, that the world I live in, that the Reality I take for granted as simply "there," is really a world that I create with the languages I use. (Paradine's conversation with Holloway makes this clear, a conversation, by the way, that has obvious connections with our talk earlier in the course about "conditioning." See Assignments 5 through 10 particularly.) This reseeing in turn helps me understand why one of the effects of education (which is a matter of my developing new languages) can be to isolate me from what I thought I knew. It helps me understand also why the process of education is so often so painful.

The fantasy of Padgett's story is simply a matter of his imagining a metaphoric truth as a literal one. Hence in Padgett's story, the fact that for different languages there are different Realities (and *vice versa*) is translated into physical terms: Scotty and Emma move quite literally from this world to another. Nonsense, which is a kind of blending of a language of this world with what seems to be a language of another world, Padgett uses to make plausible at the imaginative level not only the existence of this literal other world but the fact that moving to it is possible. (I'll go over the first stanza of "Jabberwocky" with the students in order to demonstrate how with it you can never say you "understand" what is being said any more than you can ever say you don't understand anything of what is being said: "slithy" [slimy, slippery, slithery] *seems* to suggest something you know about at the same time you can't say just what.) The effect of nonsense (before it is recognized as nonsense) is to involve a reader in the dilemma of trying to work out what in Padgett's story actually does work out—at least for Scotty and Emma. That is, as a reader of nonsense that I have not been able to name as nonsense, I am frustrated because I am hung (not hanged) between two worlds: one dead, the other powerless to be born. My old language (the way I ordinarily make sense of my Reality) won't work as I have been used to making it work (because of the way the new language has complicated it), but the new language (that which is made to look like a language by the nonsense writer who has made it up) I can't get hold of. Until I recognize that it is nonsense I'm reading, I cannot put these two languages together any more than I can forget about trying to put them together, because the suggestion of a sense to nonsense (one that I simply haven't been able to work out yet) is just too pervasive; the illusion of meaning (only a bit beyond my gropings, surely) is just too strong.

But in Padgett's story "Jabberwocky" *isn't* nonsense, and Scotty and Emma are able to make of its languages a third language which really does carry them to a new world. They become good learners. I as a reader, however, am left where I have so often found myself as a semi-student, as a would-be learner of, say, calculus who couldn't quite make it. I am in Paradine's position, looking at what I know is *not* nonsense, but with the feelings of someone who is experiencing the frustrations of nonsense unrecognized for what they are. (Paradine cannot belong to the new world; he cannot get to where his children are. Yet since they are lost to him forever, he can no longer be where he was either.) Thus for me the story becomes a way of looking at an aspect of the learning process that every learner at some point experiences (which is why, although my home felt wrong even that first Christmas vacation from college, nowhere else felt right). It dramatizes how it is that the *process* of learning is so seldom just loads of fun. Padgett's story, then, forces me to experience that the price of education is sometimes higher than I would like to believe—and that the price of the process of it, for someone in the midst of things, can sometimes feel higher than that.

26. *Edward Gorey*

Here is a story:

THE WILLOWDALE HANDCAR

BY EDWARD GOREY

OR

THE RETURN OF THE BLACK DOLL

 Afterwards a gold ring embellished with leaves, grapes, etc. was found; inside were engraved IRON HILLS and the letters D.M.G., which last stood for the words 'Don't move, Gertrude'.

Copyright © 1962 by Edward Gorey. Reprinted by permission of Robert Lantz—Candida Donadio Literary Agency, Inc.

One summer afternoon in Willowdale Edna, Harry, and Sam wandered down to the railroad station to see if anything was doing.

There was nothing on the platform but some empty crates. 'Look!' said Harry, pointing to a handcar on the siding. 'Let's take it and go for a ride.'

Soon they were flying along the tracks at a great
rate. Little Grace Sprocket, playing in a homemade mud puddle, watched them go by with
longing.

At Bogus Corners, the next town down the line,
they stopped to buy soda pop and gingersnaps
at Mr Queevil's store. 'How are things over
in Willowdale?' he asked. 'Dull' they said.

A few minutes after they were on their way again,
they saw a house burning down in a field.
'Whooee!' said Sam. 'The engines will never
be in time to save it.'

The next morning they wrote postcards to everybody, telling them what they were doing and
adding that they didn't know exactly when
they would be back.

At 10:17 the Turnip Valley Express rushed past.
A frantic face was pressed against a window
of the parlor car.

'Gracious!' said Edna. 'I believe that was Nellie
Flim. We were chums at Miss Underfoot's Seminary.
I wonder what can have been the matter.'

In Chutney Falls they hunted up the cemetery and peered at the tombstones of Harry's mother's family.

Later they ran into Nellie's beau, Dick Hammerclaw, the local telegraph operator. He asked if they'd seen her. He seemed upset.

Near Gristleburg they saw a palatial mansion on a
bluff. 'That's O Altitudo,' said Sam,'the home of
Titus W. Blotter, the financier. Come to think of it,
Nellie is his upstairs maid.'

Several days later a touring car drew up alongside
them. The driver called out something unintelligible
concerning Dick before he shot away out of sight.

An undated fragment of the 'Willowdale Triangle'
they found caught in a tie informed them that
Wobbling Rock had finally fallen on a family
having a picnic.

In Dogear Junction they paid a call on Edna's
cousins, the Zeph Claggs. He showed them a few
of the prizes from his collection of over 7,000 glass
telephone-pole insulators.

The following week Mount Smith came into view in the distance; dark clouds were piling up behind it.

During the thunderstorm that ensued, a flash of lightning revealed a figure creeping up the embankment.

Some months went by, and still they had not returned to Willowdale.

They visited the ruins of the Crampton vinegar works, which had been destroyed by a mysterious explosion the preceding fall.

At Wunksieville they rescued an infant who was hanging from a hook intended for mailbags.

'How much she resembles Nellie!' said Edna. They turned her over to the matron of the orphanage in Stovepipe City.

From the trestle over Peevish Gorge they spied the wreck of a touring car at the bottom. 'I don't see Dick's friend anywhere,' said Harry.

In Violet Springs they learned that Mrs Regera Dowdy was not receiving visitors, but through a window they were able to see the desk on which she wrote her poems.

As they were going along the edge of the Sogmush River, they passed a man in a canoe. 'If I'm not mistaken,' said Edna, 'he was lurking inside the vinegar works'.

Between West Elbow and Penetralia they almost ran over someone who was tied to the track. It proved to be Nellie.

*Despite their entreaties, she insisted on being
left at the first grade crossing, where she got
on a bicycle and rode away.*

*That evening they attended a baked-bean supper
at the Halfbath Methodist Church. 'They're
all right,' said Sam, 'but they're not a patch
on Mrs Umlaut's back home'.*

A week later they noticed someone who might have been Nellie walking in the grounds of the Weedhaven Laughing Academy.

On Sunday afternoon they saw Titus W. Blotter in his shirtsleeves plunge into the Great Trackless Swamp.

*In Hiccupboro they counted the cannon balls in
the pyramids on the courthouse lawn.*

*At sunset they entered a tunnel in the Iron Hills
and did not come out the other end.*

How do you interpret *The Willowdale Handcar?* What "happens" in the story, so far as you are concerned? What does the story seem to mean? In addressing these questions express as clearly as you can your understanding of the relationships between the various characters, between the characters and events. What do you do with such details as the Crampton vinegar works, those glass telephone-pole insulators? How about the baked-bean supper at the Halfbath Methodist Church? And the black doll (on Mrs. Regera Dowdy's desk), where does it come in? Are these Symbols? Red Herrings? Is this a story for children? For those who are Children no longer? For someone else?

However you locate yourself with these matters, bear in mind that it is two languages you are dealing with here: Gorey's use of the English language as well as the language of his drawings. Your interpretation ought to reflect how you see these two languages relating to each other. Do Gorey's drawings help you to understand what his words mean? The other way around? Or would you rather express the relation in some other way?

You have made an interpretation of *The Willowdale Handcar.* You have put things together in a certain way, arranged things so that they make sense. You have made a pattern. There is a way in which your whole life may be said to be based on the making of interpretations in very much the same way you made an interpretation of Gorey's story. Yet you do not in your life always have the same difficulty making interpretations that you did with Gorey. Nor is your attitude toward the interpretations you make always the same as your attitude toward the interpretation you have made of *The Willowdale Handcar.* Why not?

What does your experience with *The Willowdale Handcar* enable you to see in a new way, from a new angle, about the process of interpretation—and about what it means to make one?

Commentary

I'll begin by collecting the papers the students have written addressing Assignment 27.

*   *   *

As I have already indicated, I read *The Willowdale Handcar* as a work of nonsense. Its point, I think, is the offering of a performance with which to celebrate the self-control to be inferred from the kind of artistic control that has made the performance possible. By deliberately intermingling (in order to undercut) the conventions of plot and character with which we ordinarily find our ways through a story, by alternately fulfilling and upsetting our expectations of relationship and direction, and by manipulating, through his ability to mimic, the manners and rhetorics of a variety of story patterns, Gorey calls attention to the contrivance of what he has written in such a way as to focus a reader on his presence as its contriver, one whose ability to make something more than clichés out of the clichés it is playing with suggests in turn the illusion of an identity which is more than what it has built. For no matter what order a reader makes of people or events in *The Willowdale Handcar,* with whatever "because" he seeks to replace the story's "and then," he will find his order made at the expense of something in the original context, his "meaning" mocked by a suggestion of a meaning more inclusive than it is. Any attempt to bring a conventional unity or coherence to *The Willowdale Handcar* will therefore coarsen what Gorey achieves by playing off such possibilities against each other.

The most obvious "meaning" of the story, for example, the one I imagine that students will land on as the Meaning, is the seeming "story" of the eternal triangle. Nellie has been made pregnant by Titus, who seeks to dispose of her. Dick pursues Titus out of a desire to avenge Nellie's ruin. Nellie, meanwhile, has her baby but gives it up, breaks as a result of the strain she's been under, and ends up a patient in a mental institution while Dick continues to pursue Titus. But the trouble with such an interpretation is that that is all it is, a superimposition of preformed (and clichéd) patterns upon events that might just as easily be patterned differently. For Edna only "believes" it was Nellie she saw on the train; the baby merely "resembles" Nellie; the man in the canoe *may* be the man who was "lurking inside the vinegar works"; Dick *"seemed* upset"— and so on. The story is filled with such qualifications, qualifications which one is constantly tempted to forget about but does so only to have the rug yanked out from under any interpretation which fails to take them into account.

An attempt to see the story as an allegory of some sort, to make some larger symbolic meaning of it, runs into analogous difficulties. A reader can no more work Mrs. Regera Dowdy or Grace Sprocket or that baked bean supper into a story about apathy than he can work the Crampton vinegar works into a story about growing up—not without doing violence to something. It is possible to invent meanings for such details, of course, to weave a rug, but that's all that one would be doing, generalizing the specificity of the story into nothing by making 7,000 glass telephone-pole insulators a symbol of communication, for example. Yet on what principle does one *omit* such details from an interpretation of *The Willowdale Handcar?* By what logic does one say that the man in the vinegar works ("destroyed by a mysterious explosion") is "irrelevant?" Irrelevant to what? One can't do that either.

Moving to aspects of the story which might ordinarily help a reader interpret it only compounds the dilemma (compare the context of the story

Lee tells Mike in Assignment 21). Those drawings, for instance, at once so flatly clumsy and yet so wistfully graceful, so childlike and open and yet so suggestively sinister—what is the tone of them exactly, and what is to be made of it? And how does the tone of the pictures relate to the tone of Gorey's words? For the problem isn't just one of whether Wobbling Rock is part of Dick's plan for revenge or Titus's plan to shut up Nellie; it's whether a family's being squashed by something called Wobbling Rock (particularly as it is drawn) is an event a reader is supposed to laugh at or feel horrified by. A house burns down in a field. " 'Whooee!' said Sam. 'The engines will never be in time to save it.' " Is that an image of tragedy, of irresponsibility, of Gorey's having fun with a reader, or what? The three travelers enter a tunnel in the Iron Hills at sunset and don't come out the other side. Is that intended to be grim in some darkly symbolic way, or is it a parody of symbolic significances, simply a joke?

Or there is the suggestiveness of the names Gorey uses. Some of them anyway. Titus Blotter seems to equal "Tightassed Blotter" who lives way up there above the common people (and above ordinary moral decency?) in O Altitudo. But Titus is a phoney (his mansion is built on a bluff) who uses his position to seduce or soak up girls like Nellie Flim (of unformed or flimsy character), whose reputations he blots or besmirches. But to what extent is this Joycean complexity patternable? It is clear that one can see the same technique at work in Dick Hammerclaw (who is violent and rapacious?), but what does a reader do with Mr. Queevil or Dogear Junction or Wunksieville?—a question which raises in turn the question of the legitimacy of what he has already done with Blotter.

It's the same story throughout the story whatever line one tries to take into it. A reader can't say that the drawings are "no help" with the words at the same time he can't say what the "help" consists of, quite how the two go together. Plots, symbolic patterns, and tones embrace each other like Möbius curves. At every level the pedestrian melts into the bizarre only to flicker back into the seemingly normal. The illusions of relevance and irrelevance are constantly exchanging places. There is no way of putting *The Willowdale Handcar* together as we seem to be invited to put it together, and yet there is no way to stop trying to—not until one recognizes that it is nonsense he is reading. Not until one recognizes Gorey for the artist he is. This will be my way of talking about "what happens" in *The Willowdale Handcar*.

I plan to come at the latter part of the assignment by recalling one of the most important propositions that I see Padgett's story dramatizing about the relationship of language to experience. I will do this in order to talk of how I think a reader's experience with *The Willowdale Handcar* can be seen as a way of enlarging the implications of it. If Padgett's story may be seen as a way of suggesting that the worlds I live in are worlds I create with the languages I use, then I think it is possible to say that my experience with *The Willowdale Handcar,* even though it takes place at a comic level, can be said to make me aware of (by making a joke about) how often the orders I make of the world around me are distortions of the world, oversimplifications, constructs that I form less from what is "there" than from patterns that I carry around in my head (how certain I was, at one point, that I "knew" the "story" of Nellie, for example: Wealthy Financier Seduces Innocent Young Maid, when my "knowing" was really no more than a matter of my being familiar with certain soap opera clichés). *The Willowdale Handcar* explodes my attempts to apprehend it with the clichés it has seemed to invite me to use, thereby exposing me to myself as a cliché user. The joke's on me until I'm in on the joke of how this is being done and why.

But is it only my use of clichés that *The Willowdale Handcar* explodes, or is there a way in which this comic story may be said to raise a question about the use of language itself? At any rate, from the point of view that my experience with Gorey's story offers me, I can begin to see the possibility of seeing my use of language in general in another way. Yes, I use my languages to create the worlds I live in, and from this point of view they are life-giving, the way I order the chaos that I live in in order to get through a day. These languages are who I am. But to judge from my experience with Gorey, are these languages, all of them, any of them, any more than fictive fictions that for all their power to stay confusion are momentary only, no guide to truth? And what are the implications *then* of my seeing myself as a language user? For though behind the ordered chaos of *The Willowdale Handcar* there lies the creating mind of Gorey, a mind which comes to an enlightened reader as both relief and release, what lies behind the chaos of the world of experience is the point at which all language fails, and faith, if it can, must begin.

27. Seeing Other Ways of Seeing

Lewis Padgett and Edward Gorey are not the only writers to have dealt with the implications of what it means to be "conditioned to Euclid." Here is an account of the significance of the invention of a system of non-Euclidean geometry. When you come to class, know more about Lobachevsky than you can gather from the passage, and be able to supply the written source or sources for your information.

One classic example [of speculative play with logical systems] is Lobachevsky's invention of non-Euclidean geometry. . . . The new geometry . . . seemed at first mere wilful play, irresponsible in fact. The closed system of Euclidean geometry was judged to be true, not only logical in itself, but also descriptive of the nature of the space as experienced. This representative accuracy of Euclidean geometry is "true" of everyday spatial relationships in that it enables us to handle those relationships with "reasonable" accuracy. However, this "representative accuracy" is a function of traditional ways of perceiving and categorizing our experience of everyday space, traditional ways which are accepted but are neither true or untrue. Lobachevsky's invention has therefore two important consequences: 1) It questions the degree of "representative accuracy" which was traditionally attributed to the Euclidean system. Thus Lobachevsky's system tended to make the familiar strange. When we live with the familiar system without questioning it, we lose our awareness of the unfounded (even questionable) assumptions which underlie the system and our acceptance of it. We attribute a false concreteness to what in reality is only a symbolic representation, a conceptual tool. When the established system was questioned in a "strange" way by Lobachevsky the system, its assumptions, and its implications became more clear for what it was. 2) Lobachevsky's invention also makes it possible at least to conceive (if not to see) other ways of interpreting the human experience of space. Contemporary concepts of the nature of the nuclear astro-physical world would be impossible if we were still locked into the assumption that Euclidean geometry provides the final symbolic language for the expression of spatial relationships.

Language itself—mathematical symbols or words and phrases —when combined into a logical self-consistent pattern threatens constantly to deceive us as being "concrete," as not only expressing ways of thinking, but also being the way things in themselves are. This threat to constructive imagination assumed two interrelated forms:

1) over-development of expertly elaborated systems of internal consistency; 2) over-development of "apparent" and everyday concreteness. Thus Euclidean geometry, over-developed as a self-consistent system, tends to atrophy in a meaningless closed circle of expertise. Over-developed as concrete and self-evidently valid, it atrophies by becoming confused with a representative description of actual space.

—*William J. J. Gordon* *

You may never have invented a new geometry. You may never have shaped a fantasy as does Lewis Padgett. You may never have used nonsense as a way of making a joke about the "false concreteness" we attach to symbolic representations of our experience. But you have had the experience of questioning the "representative accuracy" of your way of seeing something, of becoming aware, perhaps all of a sudden, that your way of seeing something was no more than that—the expression of a way of thinking rather than "the way things in themselves are." You have also, as a consequence, been able "to conceive (if not to see) other ways of interpreting" that something.

Choose such a moment from your experience and describe it in detail. Make clear in your description what your original seeing consisted of. Make clear also what it was exactly that made you aware that your way of seeing something was no more than that. Finally, make clear what it meant to see your way of seeing as only a way of seeing. There were those other ways of seeing that you had become aware of: Were they a comfort? A horror? Of no consequence? Where were you left with your experience in this instance? What were you left with?

Commentary

I'll begin by asking the class to prepare Assignment 28 for a discussion for the next period. I'll also have the students write a paper addressing Assignment 29 which will be due that same period, and then I'll give a five minute quiz on Lobachevsky.

*   *   *

I've devised this assignment to give the students an opportunity to sort out their attitudes toward what I would call the propositional basis of both Padgett's story and *The Willowdale Handcar* about the relationship of language to experience (though the assignment you will notice, which moves out of the example of Lobachevsky's geometry as framed by the

* W. J. J. Gordon, *Synectics, op. cit.,* pp. 125–126.

quotation from Gordon, does not depend on your having taught either the Padgett or the Gorey in a certain way). In its simplest form I think this proposition would run something like this: Language is not the world; it is a way of making sense of the world. There are, however, all sorts of implications to such a proposition, and a number of ways one can feel about it—often simultaneously—when such a way of looking at things is shaped with the terms of one's life. That's what we're asking the students to shape the proposition of this assignment with, however they choose to look at it.

There is chaos in the face of which we go mad, as well as chaos we trickle lovingly through our fingers—depending. It's how a writer enacts that "depending" that I'm going to be looking for in the students' papers. I do not, in other words, care where the students claim they were "left with their experience." To see one's self, finally, as a manipulator of languages can be tragic ("My God. The truth can never be known; there is no truth"), or it can be glorious ("I with my languages make the truth for me"), or it can be both ("Though I cannot know truth, perhaps in having to make the truth I am then in turn responsible for, I can do better than know it"). Depending. But getting to the realization that one is left with no more than who he is is anything but an undramatic experience. To see a "way of seeing only as a way of seeing" implies two positions (at least), two ways of looking at things (at least), and so at least two attitudes. "Depending" involves a choice, and for a choice there has to be multiplicity. It's on the fullness and complexity with which this multiplicity is rendered, the degree of conscious awareness of the self as more than a mechanism, that I expect to be judging student papers. I can understand someone's taking an unambiguous position ultimately, but I cannot understand how someone could describe arriving at such a position without the expression of some kind of conflict.

28. The Man from Mars

Here is an opportunity for you to do some teaching. Assume that you are explaining life on this world to a Stranger from Mars. He says to you something like this:

"On New Year's Day in the Rose Bowl Northwestern University beat the University of California 20–14 before an estimated crowd of 92,000. On the next day, Sunday, the New York *Times* reported that one of the touchdowns was made as follows: 'Murakowski carried the ball to the California one-yard line and on the next play took it across.' On Monday the *Times* published a photograph of a goal line fumble that had been recovered by California. The officials had ruled that Murakowski had the ball in his possession when he crossed the goal line. In the photograph the ball is in the air and Murakowski is a yard short of the goal line. Murakowski said when shown the photograph, 'I'm sure I was across. . . . Somebody tackled me from behind and pulled me back. That's when I fumbled.'

"The same photograph shows the California tackler with his right arm stretched out, his palm held stiffly back, as if he had just driven the ball from Murakowski's arms. The ball is in the air and falling.

"Another photograph of the same play shows Northwestern Halfback Tom Worthington apparently using an illegal double stiff-arm or shove in blocking Bob Celeri, California corner back. Worthington said that he had used a high shoulder and arms block on Celeri and added that the photo must have been snapped as he was 'following through and starting to fall.'

"The newspaper reports that when the Northwestern coach boarded the Ambassador flight he said, 'It was a wonderful trip.'

"When I put all these items together," says the Martian, "they do not make sense to me. Where I come from our people are interested only in what really happens and we have no trouble learning what really happens either. In your world no one seems to know what really happened in this game."

Your problem here is to straighten out this Martian, to teach him about life in your world. In formulating a way to address him, you may care to take into consideration that the Martian is carrying a device that looks very much like a ray gun and seems in no mood for evasiveness. He expects answers that are straight and complete. Remember, this Martian is armed and dangerous. Without directness, you will be shot down. Without some ability to elaborate, you will be shot down.

Begin by making a list of items, as the Martian calls them (and what do you call them?), in this narrative, and explain how and why they do not go together, what it is the Martian means by saying that "no one seems to know what really happened in this game."

In one sense, of course, no one does know what really happened in this game. Concede this to the Martian by explaining as fully (and as graciously) as possible just how it is so.

But in another sense, we, the inhabitants of this universe, do know what happened in this game. Explain to the Martian how this is so.

You had better assume that the Martian is telling the truth when he says that his people are interested only in what really happens and that they have no trouble learning what really happens. Though you might not want to offer your conclusions to the Martian, what can you infer from his statement about what life on Mars must be like? What must learning consist of there?

But even if we assume the existence of a Man from Mars, this whole exercise is based on an impossibility, a contradiction, is it not? The Man from Mars cannot have come from the kind of world he says he does and have spoken to you so as to make you understand him. Nor could you explain anything to such a creature. Why not?

Commentary

I'll begin by collecting the papers the students have written addressing Assignment 29 and then make the last assignment of the term by asking them to write a paper addressing Assignment 30, which will be due the next period. I'll also pass back the papers the students wrote at the beginning of the course addressing Assignment 1. (These I will not have marked, by the way. On the basis of a fast reading I'll write only a single question at the bottom of each one: "A student here equals what— a victim?") Whether the students decide to use these papers for the writing of Assignment 30 or not, I'll leave to them.

*   *   *

Yes, there are all kinds of implications (and all sorts of ways that one can feel about them) to the proposition that language is not the world, but let us at least be clear, I want to have my handling of this assignment suggest, that there could be no life, and no world, as we understand either, if this were not the case. Further, that language and the world are different is not only what makes us people to begin with, it is what gives us a choice of who we are going to be. We are not Perfect Students or Martians or madmen; we are better than that because in living in a world where we have a choice of language systems to be responsible with and to, we have a chance to use language to become ourselves. Learning in our world is possible.

After Padgett, Gorey, and now Gordon on Lobachevsky, I think that this assignment ought to give the students a chance to strut their stuff a little, which I hope we can have some fun doing at the beginning of class with the first three paragraphs of directives. There is, of course, no way one could ever tell what "really happened" in the game or what the talk afterwards "really" means. No matter how many cameras from no matter how many angles were trained on the play in question, someone is going to have to determine at what point "possession" becomes "not possession," or when a momentary bobble becomes a "fumble," or when a high shoulder block becomes a "shove." At what point does a heap of rice from which one grain at a time is removed become a "heap" no longer? A man with a full head of hair from which a single hair is extracted again and again becomes "bald" when how many hairs are gone? Language does not exist to make that kind of distinction.

No matter how large one's frame of reference, the same difficulties are encountered from other perspectives. Murakowski became a hero, that's what really happened (as the Northwestern coach knew)? Or did he really blow the game (as the Northwestern coach knew)? Or was California robbed? Or did Northwestern become number one in the national ratings? Or is it simply that a lot of people got upset over nothing? No one "knows" what happened in this game because knowing in our world involves locating one's self with a language or symbol system that invariably (because it *is* a system) excludes other systems. What "really happened" in the game is a matter of someone's choosing who he is going to be (a Northwestern fan, a California rooter, someone who thinks games are silly, etc.) on the basis of what terminology he makes use of to describe what he thinks went on.

But if we understand "in this game" to refer to what took place inside the game understood as a game (and not as it may relate to anything outside itself), then of course we know "what happened" on the play in question: the fullback (or whatever position Murakowski played) scored because he was ruled to have scored. There is no possibility for another interpretation because "interpretation" in that sense does not exist inside the world of a game. This is what makes a game a game to begin with. A game is a language system in which everything can be defined: its beginnings, its proceedings, its end. Every happening is nameable; there is no event that rules cannot take care of. For there are only players in a game, no people. Every instance of a "personal foul" in a football game, for example, so far as a team is concerned, is handled in exactly the same way; savagery does not earn you more in the way of yards penalized than what may be simply a mistake (there is no "mistake" that way in a game either). "Personal foul" means just one thing (or one set of things) and what the official says is a "personal foul" is a personal foul (and what he says isn't, isn't) because the official is an "official," someone who, inside a game world, is invested with the power to act on his delegated ability to "know" in precisely the Martian's sense of the term. What he doesn't see or call didn't happen. How anyone may *feel* about an official's decision, however his decision may be seen from another point of view, is irrelevant, outside the game. A game is its own universe and is no more touched by what goes on outside it than the Dewey Decimal System is touched by someone's blowing up a library.

This is one of the best ways I can think of to talk about where it is that the Martian seems to live and why the assignment is based on a contradiction. My difficulty with trying to "teach" the Martian about life in this world is that I have no language for explaining a game to someone who lives inside one, one in which every "person" is a player and every "player" an official, as seems to be the case on Mars. It is possible for us to conceive of and establish games in our universe because our universe isn't one. We have a lot of ways of talking about "personal foul" outside the language system of a game which can change it into a number of different things. We can call it that which is for someone's own good, or inadvertent, or even a set of actions that seems demanded by national security. No one in our universe looks on Reality as it really is. Our language always means more than it says. But how do I explain a way of life to "someone" with no perspective from which to understand this? How do I detail the possibilities for the growth and change of a language user (which accompany the liabilities of his confusion and delusion) to someone whose being provides him with no way to conceive of either? I could not, presumably, explain someone who plays chess to a chess piece.

I can no more imagine what life must be like on Mars than I can imagine being able to "teach" a "someone" whose existence is based on the impossibility of learning. I might as well try to imagine a world in which black is white or where there are square triangles. The assignment is based on an impossibility because Mars and the Martian both are out of this world, beyond a universe in which language is. Someone for whom language really was the world in the way that the Martian claims it is for him could have no notion of language to begin with. He could neither frame a sentence nor understand one.

29. *The Risk of Education*

Eve—who was under the influence of a seducer, not a teacher—is perhaps the last person to have blamelessly pretended that education is a riskless experience. If a little learning is a dangerous thing, there is still some question as to whether a lot of learning is the opposite of dangerous, for a learner cannot always predict the consequences of his learning. A student cannot always foresee all of the implications of what it means to become a student. Here, for example, is a dramatization of what can happen to someone who decides to become a learner:

From the winter of 1821, when I first read Bentham, and especially from the commencement of the *Westminster Review,* I had what might truly be called an object in life; to be a reformer of the world. My conception of my own happiness was entirely identified with this object. The personal sympathies I wished for were those of fellow labourers in this enterprise. I endeavoured to pick up as many flowers as I could by the way; but as a serious and permanent personal satisfaction to rest upon, my whole reliance was placed on this; and I was accustomed to felicitate myself on the certainty of a happy life which I enjoyed, through placing my happiness in something durable and distant, in which some progress might be always making, while it could never be exhausted by complete attainment. This did very well for several years, during which the general improvement going on in the world and the idea of myself as engaged with others in struggling to promote it, seemed enough to fill up an interesting and animated existence. But the time came when I awakened from this as from a dream. It was in the autumn of 1826. I was in a dull state of nerves, such as everybody is occasionally liable to; unsusceptible to enjoyment or pleasurable excitement; one of those moods when what is pleasure at other times, becomes insipid or indifferent; the state, I should think, in which converts to Methodism usually are, when smitten by their first "conviction of sin." In this frame of mind it occurred to me to put the question directly to myself: "Suppose that all your objects in life were realized; that all the changes in institutions and opinions which you are looking forward to, would be completely effected at this very instant: would this be a great joy and happiness to you?" And an irrepressible self-consciousness distinctly answered, "No!" At this my heart sank within me: the whole foundation on which my life was constructed fell down. All my happiness was to have been found in the continual pursuit of this end. The end had ceased to charm, and how could there ever again be any interest in the means? I seemed to have nothing left to live for. . . . In vain I sought relief from my favourite books; those memorials of past nobleness and greatness from which I had always hitherto drawn strength and animation. I read them now without feeling, or with the accustomed feeling *minus* all its charms; and I became persuaded, that my love of mankind, and of excellence for its own sake, had worn itself out. . . . I frequently asked myself, if I could, or if I was bound to go on living, when life must be passed in this manner. I generally answered to myself, that I did not think I could possibly bear it beyond a year. When, however, not more than half that duration of time had elapsed, a small ray of light broke in upon my gloom. I was reading, accidentally, Marmontel's "Memoires," and came to the passage which relates his father's death, the distressed position of the family, and the sudden inspiration by which he, then a mere boy, felt and made them feel that he would be everything to them—would supply the place of all that they had lost. A vivid conception of the scene and its feelings came over me, and I was moved to tears. From this moment my burden grew lighter. The oppression of the thought that all feeling was dead within me, was gone. I was no longer hopeless: I was not a stock or a stone. I had still, it seemed, some of the material out of which all worth of character, and all capacity for happiness, are made.

—John Stuart Mill *

Mill, as you can see, is what could be called a good student, a good learner. Yet had he not created from the language systems of Bentham and the *Westminster Review* a language of his own with which to see the world, would he have had to experience the depression that he did? If he had not got into the pernicious habit of putting questions to himself, would he have had any trouble? It is true that Mill seems to have made something of a recovery, but that was just an accident, wasn't it? Mill was just lucky?

*   *   *

Where do you find yourself with what could be called the risk of education?

Though we all believe that it is a good thing to change one's mind, though in our ordinary talk about education the open mind is praised, the closed mind condemned, there are parts of the present, and future, about which we are already decided, about which, like Mill, none of us intend to change if we can help it. What sort of person would believe that you should change your mind all the time about everything indefinitely?

* *The Autobiography of John Stuart Mill,* "A Crisis in My Mental History," 1873.

But to judge from Mill's experience, it is sometimes difficult to help it. It is difficult to know the limits of an idea.

Write a paper in which you state a belief that you do not intend to change your mind about. Since this is a belief you will be talking about, no one can argue with you about it with propriety (this does not mean that no one can comment on the sentence or paragraph structure of what you write). State your belief and then deal with the following questions.

What safeguards are you taking to protect this belief? Are there certain discussions you just turn away from? Is there evidence you simply refuse to consider? What exactly are your defenses? How do you use them?

But no matter how intricate your defenses, they may not be adequate, not if you intend to become a student. Using your particular belief as an example, explain just why this is so.

It is, of course, possible for someone to associate himself with an educational institution, with the educational process, without attempting to become a student. Yet many do make this attempt, many people who believe in what they believe in just as strongly as you believe in what you believe in. What do you imagine would make the risk of education worth running for such people? Or is it that they are ignorant of the fact that they are running a risk? All of them? All of us?

Speaking just for yourself, knowing what you know, do you think it worth it for you to attempt to become a student?

Commentary

I'll begin class by collecting the papers the students have written addressing Assignment 30.

*　　*　　*

I trust it is obvious why most of what I have to say about my expectations for the last four or five writing assignments of the course translates in one way or another into a hope for honesty of self-confrontation on the part of the students, a hope for complexity and depth. It is true that we advertise Assignment 30 as "the last paper" the students will write for the course and offer it as an opportunity "to put some things together." But any one of these last writing assignments, as the wording of them is intended to suggest, might easily be considered an opportunity for the students in the same way: a chance for someone to put some things together that will enable him to put himself together in a way that has meaning to him. I don't think we have ever invited students to do anything less or anything else (the assignments with which we opened the term, from where we are now, may be seen to be just as complicated as what we have been dealing with recently), but the students, some of them anyway, are hearing us differently now; they are not what they were and neither are we. Thus in these last four or five writing assignments we are able to make the honesty of self-confrontation, the complexity and depth with which the students choose to see their experience, *the* issue of the paper in a way that we couldn't have earlier—not and have expected what I think we have a right to expect of the students at this point in the course. "Over to you, now," we're saying unmistakably; "how do you see the relevance of this problem to your life as you are living it? Or, as you'd like to?" To address such questions, as we have good reason to know, can be a meaningful activity only when one has some sense of what he is doing. And as we also have good reason to know, this is a sense that has to be developed. We've earned the right, I think, to be making the demands that we are.

What I will be looking for in Assignment 29, then, is poignancy to students' rendering of their understanding of the position they assume as learners. When I assign the paper, I will suggest they use the Mill passage as they did the passage by Dundas on Assignment 18. It cannot serve the students as a model other than to dramatize that the risk of education is perhaps a more complex issue than might first be imagined. For to judge from Mill's account of his experience, it is not so simple as saying that the risk of education is that you may change your mind about a couple of ideas (what happens to Mill is a good deal more serious than that), but that the risk is worth taking because there is a good chance that other ideas will come along to replace them (Marmontel's "Memoires" do not just "come along," nor are they what saved Mill). That way of putting things (though I suppose some of our students are going to talk on just such a level) is what I would call the almost right that is wronger than wrong. It is, of course, an "idea" that could be said to be responsible for Mill's depression, but the focus of the assignment is on what led Mill to entertain the idea as an idea to begin with. It was, I think, the habit of being a good learner, which in Mill's case involved not only the putting of languages together (from the language systems of Bentham and *The Westminster Review*), but a questioning of the value of those languages in terms of who he was as a person. In other words, what threw Mill into a depression was not his discovering the inadequacy of the language he had developed for "reform" to do what he had been doing with it (his means he never questions that way, and his ends, his "objects in life," he seems always to have been aware were incapable of "complete attainment"); it was the flash of insight attending his seeing his "objects in life" in two different ways simultaneously, as "ends" which for all their abstract value he could no longer find himself believing in, heart and mind, in the way that he once had. In losing how he felt about the language he had developed, Mill lost the way he had located himself. In losing his means of self-location (like Paradine in Padgett's story, like Hadley after his experience in the bar but before his conversion, like the reader of nonsense who does not know it is nonsense he is reading), Mill lost who he was.

But it is this same learning habit that saves Mill, his constant (and anything but "vain") seeking for "relief" (for what he could make into a language he could believe in, a language that would again give him back himself). For though Mill's reading of Marmontel may have been an accident (and his response to it mysterious), what Mill *told* himself his response to Marmontel meant, and the meaning he went on to make of that meaning, was not an accident. It is the kind of thing that could have "happened" only to someone who was continuing to act like a learner (whether he knew it or not), only to someone continuing to behave as though the learning process could have something to do with who he wanted to be (whether he believed it or not).

Or so I read the passage. It is enough if students see it as no more than a way of suggesting that the matter of this assignment is serious and that our questions are wide open.

30. *Putting Things Together*

From cradle to grave this problem of running order through chaos, direction through space, discipline through freedom, unity through multiplicity, has always been and must always be, the task of education. . . . At the utmost, the active-minded young man should ask of his teacher only mastery of his tools. The young man himself, the subject of education, is a certain form of energy; the object to be gained is economy of his force; the training is partly the clearing away of obstacles, partly the direct application of effort. Once acquired, the tools and models may be thrown away.°

*　　*　　*

This is the last paper you will write for this course. It is an opportunity for you to put some things together for yourself, whatever it is you care to connect in whatever order you choose.

Imagine someone who has just read over everything you have read for this course this term saying something like this to you:

"What does it mean exactly that the real subject of this course is language, but that the metaphor used to talk about it is teaching and learning? What does teaching and learning have to do with language? *Your* learning specifically? And what does this have to do with your writing? Are you supposed to have become a writer or what?"

Write a paper in which you attempt to answer him.

You might begin by rereading the materials of the course yourself. You may also wish to recall conversations you have had about the course or in it. Most important, you will want to read back over your own work, for it is not *a* course you are going to be talking about in this paper, but *your* course. It is not the experience of a *we* (either supposed or actual) that this someone is interested in, but *your* experience, the experience of an *I*, of another someone. For this reason you might therefore wish to consider whether you are sure that you want to say obvious things such as "My writing has improved" (or "failed to improve"). Do you really want to bother with trying to guess what you think someone else wants you to say? Do you really want to bother at this point with the clichés? But how are you going to say that you're better than, or worse than, or just the same as you were without simply asking someone to take your word for it?

° *The Education of Henry Adams,* 1906.

Suppose you aren't the writer that you want to be? Does this mean that your time has been wasted? That you wasted your time? Any other possibilities?

Perhaps it would be possible to handle these matters in terms of a situation, in terms of a specific instance of teaching or learning where people did things, moved and talked?

A good place to begin thinking out a way to address the problem of this paper might be to consider specifically the first paper you wrote for the course which has just been returned to you. Who were you in that paper? Who are you now? Have you changed your mind about anything? What is there you haven't changed your mind about?

Commentary

I guess there's no getting around my having to say that this assignment brings us full circle, which I phrase in the tentative way that I do in part to prepare myself for the fact that the students' final papers will probably not be anywhere near so good as I think they should be. But if we really believe one of the main assumptions with which we began the course, that teaching and learning finally are worth no more than they can be made to mean, then not only can this not be helped, but I think we have to accept it as one of the inevitable consequences of our having attempted what we have. How could the students' papers be what I think they ought to be? And why should they be what I think they should? We have to be careful here not to use this as a way of overlooking where we may have failed students as teachers, but at the same time I think it important to bear in mind that there are ways in which we haven't failed them.

We have worked together to create a set of writing assignments and class exercises that have as their audience the best of what we believe students capable. We have allowed them to choose what use they would make of what we have made available to them. No teacher, so far as I'm concerned, can do more than this and remain a teacher. No teacher can do less and be one. It is fitting, then, that in this final paper we offer the students the opportunity to say for themselves only what they can say for themselves about where they have been, what they have come from, and where they are going. We are asking students here not to say what they think they learned, but to show what they did. There is a great difference. For better or for worse, then, this final paper, in being the expression of what each individual has made his experience with the course mean to him, will be the expression also of each individual's understanding of himself as a language user. It will be on the quality of that awareness enacted as a statement that I will judge what my students write.

But it is important to remember also that it is a circle we have sought to close with these assignments, not a Grand Conclusion we have been marching to or some kind of final Epiphany we have demanded that our students seek. Our end is but the illumination of where we started. So from another perspective, this final paper is only one more paper in a sequence of papers, the whole of which is more important than any single part—and important as an action, as a process that we see only the beginning of. How a given student performs on this one paper is not necessarily a measure of what he has made the course mean to him or of what he has learned, one way or the other—not any more than how our students perform on this one paper can be the sole measure of either what we have taught or the value of it. That some students will display what we might choose to call very little awareness of themselves as language users—now, on this paper, at this point in time and in those terms—I don't think is necessarily the full story of an educational experience constructed to begin only at its conclusion.

For though we have to be careful here, too, one of the things I would say that our work this term has made me aware of is that the meaning of learning must be acknowledged (even if it cannot be judged) in terms of what it has the potential to involve as well as in terms of what it does— which is as true for what we have given the students to work with as it is for whatever they have done with it. We have not turned students into writers; no course does that and no course can. But in devising a syllabus to raise and clarify problems that no educational process can proceed without reference to, we have made available to them what they can grow to as well as with. In seeing writing as involving the workings of language in the way that we have tried to, we have provided students with a way of seeing what there can be *in* the activity of writing for anyone who seeks to involve himself with it. And in leaving to students, as Agassiz did, the responsibility of devising a language for whatever they care to make this mean, we have offered them a chance to belong to themselves. Our course is finished. What we may have started with it will need time to begin.